THE
RUNNER'S WORLD
COOKBOOK

150 ULTIMATE RECIPES
FOR FUELING UP AND
SLIMMING DOWN—
WHILE ENJOYING EVERY BITE

Edited by **Joanna Sayago Golub**

RODALE.

Some of the recipes were previously published in *Runner's World* magazine and on runnersworld.com. For a full list of contributors, see page 265.

© 2013 by Rodale Inc.

Rodale books may be purchased for business or promotional use or for special sales. For information, please write to: Special Markets Department, Rodale, Inc., 733 Third Avenue, New York, NY 10017

Runner's World is a registered trademark of Rodale Inc.

Printed in the United States of America

Rodale Inc. makes every effort to use acid-free ♾, recycled paper ♻.

Book design by Christina Gaugler

Photography by Mitch Mandel

Library of Congress Cataloging-in-Publication Data is on file with the publisher.

ISBN-13: 978–1–62336–168–6 direct hardcover

ISBN-13: 978–1–62336–123–5 trade hardcover

Distributed to the trade by Macmillan

4   6   8   10   9   7   5   direct hardcover

8   10   9   7   trade hardcover

We inspire and enable people to improve their lives and the world around them.
rodalebooks.com

For *my mom and dad,*
who taught me the joys
of cooking for and with family

Contents

FOREWORD

Running and cooking are my two greatest passions—and not necessarily in that order. I started running when I was 11 years old, and it's no coincidence that my love of food and cooking began nearly simultaneously. I was intrigued by the relationship between training and the food I ate. As athletes, we expend energy while running and need to support our bodies' needs with nutrient-rich choices. I learned, for example, how adding a cucumber to my salad after a hot summer run could help cool my core temperature (for a great cooling recipe, try the Cantaloupe and Cucumber Salad on page 77). I came to believe—and still do—that if you enhance the quality of your food, the quality of your running will be equally enhanced.

When I was on the island of Crete training for the 2004 Athens Olympic Marathon, I felt firsthand how eating quality food could support a rigorous training schedule. The watermelon and vegetables we ate at lunch were grown on the estate we stayed at, as were the cured olives that accompanied every meal. These same olives were pressed to make the oil we used to dip our locally baked bread, and the lamb served at dinner was raised on the farm next door. These foods fueled my training, helping me become the first American to medal in the Olympic Marathon since Joan Benoit Samuelson took gold in the 1984 Olympic games in Los Angeles. I have also experienced how poor food choices, often for convenience's sake, can leave me feeling tired and irritable, leading to a disappointing workout or race.

I'm not only interested in food because of its effect on training, but I'm also interested in it because of the relationships it can help build with friends, teammates, and family. And for me, those relationships are everything. There have been some seriously brilliant runners from around the world who have dined at our kitchen table (in our house, there's really no need for a living room because we tend to spend all our time around the table) and shared in profound conversations. American record holders, world champions, Olympic medalists, and national champions by the dozens have come to refuel after a long run or dine late into an evening after a hard day of training.

The Runner's World Cookbook can help you accomplish these dual goals—creating meals made with simple ingredients that fuel your training while helping build relationships with those you love. The book contains some of the best recipes ever published in *Runner's World* magazine and were created by great chefs, nutritionists, and runners. These recipes will satisfy, empower, and keep you running optimally—while meeting any dietary need or craving you have. You may be the type of person who can eat breakfast at any meal. Or perhaps you're looking for a fast and simple recipe. You may need vegetarian or gluten-free options. Or maybe you're like me and love to experiment and challenge yourself with new ingredients. You'll find all of these options here in this book.

Like so many runners, I train hard, run a business, chase after my daughter, walk the dog, and try to keep up with my tireless husband. I need food that will sustain me. At the end of the day when my work is complete, I bring my friends, family, and teammates together in the kitchen to share in a meal intended to nourish and satisfy everyone at the table. Yes, training makes us better athletes, but not without also eating good food that strengthens our bodies and the bonds with those around us. In that sense, maybe, just maybe, this book is all you need to set a new kind of personal best.

Deena Kastor
2004 Olympic Marathon Bronze Medalist
American Marathon and Half-Marathon Record Holder

PREFACE:
what it means to eat like a runner

Runners love to eat. In fact, it's the reason why many of us at *Runner's World* run in the first place—and chances are, it's partially the reason why you run, too. Logging all those miles (and burning all those calories) allows you to enjoy food in a way that nonrunners can't understand. First, we enjoy all the *good* it does for our bodies. Healthy, well-balanced meals offer our tired muscles the nutrients they need to heal, refuel, and grow stronger. This is important so that we can perform better during tomorrow's workout, as well as stay healthy and continue running strong for years to come. But runners also appreciate eating *well*. We want—and have earned the right—to enjoy delicious, well-prepared meals that feel indulgent, even if they're not. And if the occasional meal is on the indulgent side, well, that's okay because we've earned the right to eat those meals, too.

That philosophy—that you can eat well while fueling your body—is something we strive to bring to the pages of *Runner's World* every month. Over the years, we've published hundreds of recipes that show you how to create nutrient-rich and satisfyingly delicious meals that you can cook for yourself, your family, and your friends. Now we've compiled the very best of those recipes into one cookbook that you can turn to no matter your needs. Looking for the ideal prerun meal to fuel your workout or a high-protein recovery dish? We've got both covered—just look for the easy-to-spot "Prerun" or "Recovery" label at the top of each recipe. Or skim the Special Recipe Lists on pages 257 to 264 for meals that fit either category. Runners trying to lose weight will be happy to know that more than 100 of our recipes contain 400 calories or less and are labeled "Low-Calorie." And if you're among the many runners with special dietary needs, we provide plenty of recipes that are vegetarian, vegan, or gluten-free.

We know how important it is for a recipe to be easy to follow, reliable, and fast. That's why every recipe has gone through the rigors of the Test Kitchen at Rodale (*Runner's World*'s parent company) to ensure each one comes out just right every time—and often in 30 minutes or less. Getting a meal on the table that fast is something every runner can appreciate, because as much as we enjoy healthy, delicious food, we enjoy having extra time to spend on the road or trail, taking part in the pastime that allows us the freedom to eat exactly how we want.

—Joanna Sayago Golub
Senior Editor
Runner's World

INTRODUCTION:
how to eat like a runner

Whether you run 10 miles a week or 100, are a meat-eater or a vegan, or are a seasoned cook or kitchen newbie, as a runner you should keep certain key nutrition tenets in mind. Using these four overarching philosophies as your daily guide will ensure that your diet provides all the essential nutrients you need for strong running and good health. And, not coincidentally, if you follow these tenets, you'll discover that the food you prepare for yourself, your family, and your friends will taste unbelievably fresh, wholesome, and—most important—delicious. Here's how to make every meal and snack worth biting into.

1. eat a rainbow of produce every day

You already know that eating fruits and vegetables supplies your body with the vitamins, minerals, and carbs you need to fuel your running. But to get the most from your produce, you need to think in terms of color—red, orange, yellow, green, blue, purple. There are 400-plus pigments that light up the supermarket produce aisle, and they each offer unique benefits. You'll find fruits and vegetables in every health-boosting shade throughout this cookbook.

The rich red in pomegranate comes from anthocyanins, the deep red in tomatoes from lycopene, and the bright orange in sweet potatoes from beta-carotene. These and other pigments have been shown to lower your risk of cancer, heart disease, and Alzheimer's, while also improving your memory. And since most pigments act as antioxidants, they can help reduce inflammation caused by disease or heavy exercise. But studies suggest that the pigments in produce need to interact with other color compounds in fruits or vegetables to produce their beneficial effects, which is why it's important to eat a wide variety of colors every day. The results of these studies also explain why taking a single pigment, such as beta-carotene, in supplement form doesn't lead to the same health improvements as eating the whole foods and may even increase your risk for some diseases.

Runners should aim for nine total servings each day of colorful fruits and vegetables

Chase the Rainbow

THESE COLORFUL PRODUCE PICKS PACK ANTIOXIDANTS AND NUTRIENTS THAT RUNNERS NEED

RED

Beets
Nitrates found in beets may make your muscles work more efficiently during exercise by reducing the amount of oxygen they need.

Try it Beets with Avocado and Orange, page 78

Tomatoes
Their red pigment is a result of high levels of lycopene, an antioxidant that may reduce your risk for certain cancers and protect against ultraviolet damage caused by running in the sun.

Try it Fire-Roasted Meat Sauce, page 139

YELLOW AND ORANGE

Mangoes
High vitamin C intake may reduce upper respiratory tract infections, as well as help lower your heart rate during exercise. One cup of mango delivers 75 percent of your daily need for C.

Try it Chicken-Mango Fajitas, page 180

Sweet potatoes
One sweet potato provides more than three times your daily need for immune-boosting vitamin A in the form of beta-carotene. It's also full of carbohydrates to keep a runner's energy stores topped up.

Try it Jerk Shrimp with Sweet Potato and Black Beans, page 203

GREEN

Kale
This leafy green is jam-packed with vitamin C, vitamin K, and vision-protecting beta-carotene. Add it to soups, salads, and sandwiches.

Try it Warm Butternut Squash and Kale Salad, page 221

Avocadoes
Nearly 70 percent of the fat found in this fruit is monounsaturated—the same kind that makes olive oil especially heart-healthy. Half an avocado also delivers 7 grams of fiber.

Try it Thai Avocado Soup, page 90

BLUE AND PURPLE

Eggplant
Eggplant, which has just 20 calories per cup, contains antioxidants with heart-protective qualities.

Try it Grilled Vegetable Polenta Casserole, page 219

Blackberries
These superfruits have about twice as much antioxidant power as blueberries, raspberries, and strawberries. Consuming plenty of antioxidants may reduce postworkout muscle tissue damage, speed recovery, and boost immune function.

Try it Blackberry Dressing, page 86

WHITE

Bananas
This runner favorite brims with potassium and quick-digesting carbs. Potassium plays a key role in muscle contraction, with low levels linked to muscle cramping.

Try it Banana-Oat Energy Bars, page 47

Celeriac
What it lacks in aesthetics, celeriac (a knobby-looking root vegetable also called celery root) makes up for with stellar amounts of vitamin K—a single cup packs 80 percent of your daily need.

Try it Celeriac and Potato Soup, page 99

(a serving equals a medium-size piece of fruit, ⅓ cup of dried fruit, 1 cup of raw vegetables, ½ cup of cooked vegetables, or 2 cups of salad greens). While that may sound like a lot, you shouldn't have any trouble hitting that mark with our fruit- and-vegetable-packed recipes. These appear not only in Chapter 9 on Vegetables but also throughout the cookbook. Check the Special Recipe Lists on pages 261 to 263 for vegetarian and vegan recipes that particularly emphasize produce. Select different colored fruits and vegetables, with a goal of eating five unique colors daily. Keep in mind, too, that frozen fruits and vegetables are just as healthy as fresh and are often more convenient. For that reason, many of our recipes call for frozen produce, but fresh can just as easily be used.

And whenever possible, eat the peel (most of our recipes call to leave the peel on unless doing so has a significant effect on the quality of the finished dish). Plants' outer skins protect them from UV light, parasites, and other invaders. As a result, those skins are bursting with a wide range of phytochemicals that protect your health. Produce skin is also rich in resistant starches and various types of fiber. These compounds promote the growth of healthy bacteria in the intestines, improve intestinal function, help curb appetite, and aid in weight control—reasons good enough to put down the peeler.

2. choose the right carbohydrates

Runners require more carbohydrates than the average person, especially in the days leading up to a marathon or other endurance race. After all, carbohydrates are the body's top choice for fuel and the best energy source for working muscles. In general, runners should be taking in about 50 to 65 percent of their calories in the form of carbohydrates (the higher your mileage, the higher your percentage should be). That won't be a problem with all of the carb-packed recipes found throughout this cookbook—not just in Chapter 6 on Pasta and Sauces. But not all carbs are created equal. And for runners, whole grain carbohydrates are almost always the best choice.

Whole grain foods are made from the entire grain, including the bran, the germ, and the endosperm. It's within the whole grain that you'll find nutritious B vitamins, iron, magnesium, selenium, and fiber. Whole grains' high fiber content slows carbohydrate digestion, releasing glucose into the bloodstream at a slower rate for long, sustained energy. It also keeps you fuller longer, helps control your weight, reduces cholesterol levels, and improves heart health.

When whole grains are milled into refined grains, the bran and the germ—and the nutrients they pack—are lost. Lots of refined carbohydrates are fortified to add back some of the nutrients, but you can't add back all the fiber. For these many health reasons, we emphasize throughout the cookbook using whole grain options whenever possible—from whole grain sandwich bread, to brown rice, to less common grains like farro. While many of these whole grains contain gluten (a protein found in wheat, barley, and

Kernels of Health

NUTRIENT-PACKED WHOLE GRAINS ARE GOOD FOR YOUR RUNNING—AND YOUR TASTEBUDS

Amaranth

Rich in iron and fiber, 1 cooked cup of these tiny seeds contains just over 9 grams of protein.

Try It Stir cooked amaranth into the batter of Hearty Whole Grain Muffins (page 16) or Multigrain Pancakes (page 26), or use it to make a hot porridge.

Barley

Research suggests that the fiber in barley may lower cholesterol more effectively than oat fiber.

Try It The recipe for Mediterranean Pork-Asparagus Stir-Fry (page 173) uses barley as a chewy, flavorful alternative to white rice.

Brown Rice

Easy-to-digest brown rice is rich in fiber, minerals, and vitamins. One cooked cup supplies more than 100 percent of your daily need for manganese.

Try It Stove-Top Pork and Brown Rice (page 171) makes for a hearty one-pot meal on a cold night.

Bulgur

Bulgur, which has twice as much fiber as brown rice, is made from wheat kernels that have been boiled, dried, and coarsely ground.

Try It Try *Runner's World* contributing food writer Mark Bittman's fresh-tasting Tabbouleh (page 80) for a dish that pairs bulgur with parsley, mint, and lemon.

Corn

Gluten-free, carb-rich corn is often mistaken as being nutrient poor, but actually has nearly twice the antioxidant activity found in apples.

Try It Stick-with-You Polenta (page 25) makes a hearty breakfast packed with antioxidant-rich dried fruits and nuts.

Farro

This Italian staple is a good source of magnesium, B vitamins, and vitamin E.

Try It Caprese Farro Salad (page 83) pairs this plump, chewy whole grain with tomatoes, mozzarella, and basil.

Oats

A favorite of runners, oats are rich in a type of fiber called beta-glucan, which may play a role in strengthening the immune system.

Try It As the recipe for Steel Cut Oatmeal Risotto with Asparagus (page 217) shows, you can make this Italian comfort dish with any whole grain.

Quinoa

This powerhouse offers about 8 grams of protein in every cooked cup. It's also a rich source of the amino acid lysine, which aids tissue repair.

Try It Heating quinoa in a dry skillet, as is done in Swiss Chard with Toasted Quinoa and Tomato (page 227), brings out its earthy, nutty flavor.

Spelt

This high-fiber wheat substitute contains more protein than common wheat.

Try It Look for spelt pasta at the supermarket and use it instead of rigatoni in Rigatoni with Chicken Sausage (page 158).

Teff

A staple in Ethiopian runners' diets, this tiny, iron-rich grain is a good source of calcium and fiber.

Try It Use teff in place of oats in Creamy Cocoa Oatmeal (page 21).

Bread and Pasta Buying Guide

LOOK FOR WHOLE GRAINS

Whole wheat, brown rice, buckwheat, spelt, or other whole grains should appear first in the ingredient list. "Semolina flour" (which is used to make traditional pasta) and "enriched wheat flour" are both code words for refined flour, which lacks the nutrients of whole grains. If there's a label on the package that says the product is made from 100 percent whole grains, that's even better.

CHECK THE FIBER CONTENT

Whole grain pasta and bread should provide 5 grams of fiber or more per serving (a serving of pasta is 2 ounces; a serving of bread is one slice).

LOOK FOR PROTEIN

Whole grains naturally contain protein, which will help jump-start muscle recovery postrun. A 2-ounce serving of pasta and one slice of bread should both provide 5 to 6 grams of protein.

rye), plenty do not. That's good news if you're one of the many runners who need to avoid gluten. For a list of gluten-free recipes featuring wholesome wheat alternatives, see the Special Recipe Lists on pages 263 to 264.

As healthy as whole grains are, refined carbohydrates can play a role in a runner's diet. In the days just before a race, eating low-fiber, easily digested carbohydrates, such as traditional pasta, white rice, and bagels, will provide your body with the quickly absorbed energy you need to fuel your muscles—without risk of upsetting your stomach. That's why you'll find recipes in Chapter 6 that use traditional pasta. And, of course, if a recipe calls for whole grain pasta, you can always swap it out for the traditional version if preferred. But more often than not, whole grains—and foods made from them—should be the staple carbohydrate of your diet. Health benefits aside, whole grains simply taste better. They offer much more interesting texture and rich, full flavor that their refined counterparts simply can't match.

3. get the right fats

Runners have had an uneasy relationship with fat over the years. Because we want to stay lean to run strong, our tendency is to avoid having too much fat in our diet. And generally, that's a good thing, since consuming too much fat can lead to weight gain. But runners took that fat-phobic tendency to the extreme in the 1990s, when the national fat-free craze was at its peak and foods like fat-free salad dressing, reduced-fat peanut butter, and even fat-free cookies were popular. Did the fact that these foods contain little or no fat mean they were better for you? As we've clearly learned since then, absolutely not.

Fat is an essential part of a runner's diet. It plays a key role in maintaining general good health and in boosting performance. Skimping on fat can leave you hungry, injury-prone, and deficient in key vitamins and minerals (see below for more details on those effects)—none of which will help you set a new personal record. The key is to make sure you're eating the right kinds of fats. Trans fats, which are more often found in processed foods, are extremely harmful because they raise your levels of low-density lipoprotein (LDL or so-called "bad cholesterol") while simultaneously lowering your high-density lipoprotein (HDL or so-called "good cholesterol"). This significantly increases your risk for heart disease, stroke, and type 2 diabetes, not to mention your risk of packing on pounds. Your goal should be to eliminate most or all trans fats from your diet, and the best way to do that is to avoid heavily processed foods.

Saturated fats, which are largely found in meat and dairy, are also generally considered a less-than-healthy choice because they, too, can raise LDL. However, as new research is showing, not all saturated fats are bad—some, like stearic acid and lauric acid, may not be harmful at all and could even potentially hold health benefits. That said, current dietary recommendations advise keeping your saturated fat intake to around 16 grams or fewer per day (based on a 2,000-calorie diet). That's why throughout the cookbook, we emphasize choosing lean cuts of red meat and poultry and low-fat or fat-free milk, yogurt, and cheeses. (In recipes calling for low-fat milk, the nutritional analysis was done with 2% milk, but you could use 1%.) When butter, a source of saturated fats, is called for, it's because it's needed to create a desired texture or flavor that other fats can't duplicate. But it's always used in moderation.

The fats runners want and need in their diets are unsaturated fats. These include mono- and polyunsaturated fats. While both types of unsaturated fats are found in many foods, monounsaturated fats, which have heart-protective qualities, are typically found in vegetable oils, such as olive oil, canola oil, and sesame oil (see "Liquid Gold" on page 7 for uses for these oils and more). Other sources include avocados, nuts and

Liquid Gold

A GUIDE TO USING HEALTHY OILS

BEST FOR COLD PREPARATIONS

Extra-Virgin Olive Oil

Rich, slightly peppery-tasting extra-virgin olive oil is minimally processed, so it retains extremely high levels of antioxidants, including vitamin E and a compound called oleocanthal. This compound has anti-inflammatory properties similar to ibuprofen and may help reduce inflammation in the body over time. You can also use it for cooking, though doing so diminishes its antioxidants.

Keep it fresh When exposed to light and air, antioxidants in extra-virgin olive oil can start to break down. To preserve its health benefits, store the oil in a dark glass container or tin in a cool, dark place.

Try it Drizzle a fragrant, flavorful extra-virgin olive oil over the Caramelized Onion and Fig Pizza (page 133) just before serving.

Flaxseed Oil

Flaxseed oil contains more inflammation-reducing omega-3s than fish oil and is one of the few vegetarian sources of the nutrient. Research shows that omega-3 fatty acids may help alleviate and possibly prevent joint pain and prevent exercise-induced asthma.

Keep it fresh Flaxseed oil goes rancid quickly, so store it in the refrigerator. Heat diminishes its omega-3s. Use it solely in cold preparations.

Try it Rather than tossing popcorn in butter, drizzle it with flaxseed oil. Try it on Cinnamon and Sugar Popcorn (page 49). Or add a teaspoon or two to any smoothie (pages 56 to 61).

Walnut Oil

Aside from flaxseed oil, walnut oil is one of the few concentrated plant sources of omega-3 fatty acids. Studies have shown that omega-3s in walnuts and walnut oil help reduce the body's biological response to stress. Good news, since people who have extreme responses to stress are at higher risk for heart disease.

Keep it fresh Opened walnut oil lasts for 6 to 12 months. To prevent it from going rancid, store it in the refrigerator or in a cabinet away from heat.

Try it Nutty Olive Oil Dressing (page 86) gets an omega-3 boost from walnut oil.

BEST FOR COOKING

Canola Oil

Canola oil has a light, neutral flavor and the least amount of saturated fat of all cooking oils. One tablespoon contains 14 percent of your daily need for vitamin E. Large amounts of this nutrient aren't found in many fruits and vegetables, so a heart-healthy source like canola oil is a good way to get it into your diet.

Keep it fresh Save money by buying canola oil in bulk. When stored in a cool, dark cupboard, it's shelf-stable for about a year, even after being opened.

Try it This inexpensive oil has a high smoke point, making it ideal for stir-fries like Thai Beef and Snow Pea Stir-Fry (page 168). Its mild taste also makes it a good substitute for some of the butter used in quick breads and muffins.

Avocado Oil

Light, buttery avocado oil is rich in heart-healthy monounsaturated fat. It also contains phytochemicals that may lessen ultraviolet-induced cellular damage—good news for runners who log their miles in the sun.

Keep it fresh When stored in the refrigerator, avocado oil will last 9 to 12 months.

Try it Avocado oil has the highest smoke point of any plant oil, making it ideal for high-heat cooking like Grilled Asparagus (page 222), but its mild, buttery flavor is just as delicious in pesto. Swap it in for the olive oil in Cilantro-Pumpkin Pesto (page 143).

Sesame Oil

Nutty sesame oil consists of nearly equal parts mono- and polyunsaturated fats. Research shows that using sesame oil in place of other oils may help reduce blood pressure and blood sugar levels in people with diabetes, possibly due to the oil's antioxidant content.

Keep it fresh Use sesame oil within 3 to 6 months of opening and store it away from direct light and heat.

Try it Light sesame oil has a high smoke point, ideal for cooking and stir-fries. But it also adds a nutty flavor to fresh vegetable dishes like Fresh Market Slaw (page 75). Dark sesame oil, which has an intense, smoky flavor, is better for drizzling over finished dishes.

seeds, and nut butters. Peanut butter is a favorite food of runners, and if you've never tried almond butter or cashew butter, you're in for a treat. Be sure to earmark the recipes for our Almond Butter and Pear Sandwich (page 134) and Cashew Butter and Mango Chutney Sandwich (page 41) to try later.

Like monounsaturated fats, polyunsaturated fats are found in oils and have heart-protective qualities. They can also reduce your risk for type 2 diabetes. Omega-3s, which have inflammation-reducing qualities, are a type of polyunsaturated fat found in abundance in fatty fish, such as salmon, sardines, and anchovies (all three of which you'll find recipes for in Chapter 8 on Fish and Seafood Mains), and some nuts like walnuts and flaxseeds. Runners should aim to make 30 percent of their calories come from these healthy unsaturated fats. That's a pretty big chunk of your diet. But given that 1 gram of fat contains 9 calories (compared to the 4 calories found in 1 gram of carbohydrate or protein), it won't be difficult to meet. If you still need more reasons to add good-for-you unsaturated fats to your diet, read on.

Keep you satisfied Unsaturated fats reduce hunger, give you that satisfied feeling after a meal, and minimally impact blood sugar. That's important because if your blood sugar dips too low, you may be more inclined to crave less-than-healthy foods and to overeat. Low blood sugar also leaves you feeling low on energy, in a daze, and far from being able to run your best.

Help absorb nutrients Many vitamins, including A, D, E, and K, and antioxidant compounds are best absorbed when eaten with fats. This means by choosing that fat-free salad dressing, you're missing out on a boatload of key nutrients. Our salads in Chapter 3 use plenty of healthy oils that will boost nutrient absorption so you get the most out of your meal.

Protect heart health As explained earlier, unsaturated fats found in vegetable oils (such as olive and canola), avocados, and nuts have the power to help lower LDL and reduce your risk of heart disease.

Reduce injury Research shows that consuming unsaturated fats may help stave off injuries, including stress fractures. One reason for this may be that fat helps your body absorb vitamin D, a nutrient that plays a key role in strengthening bones.

Decrease joint pain Omega-3 fatty acids (found in salmon, walnuts, and flaxseed) possess anti-inflammatory properties that can help soothe knee, back, and joint aches and pains that plague many runners. Translation: Eat more omega-3s, hurt less, and run more.

4. meet your protein needs

Protein is essential for a healthy runner's body—for more reasons than you might realize. This key nutrient helps preserve lean mass and build new muscle tissue after a strenuous run, which can cause microscopic tears and damage to muscle fibers. In fact, studies show that runners who consume the right amount of protein are less likely to get injured (because their muscles heal faster) than those who skimp.

But that's not the only reason why you need protein. High protein intake has also been shown to help maintain a strong immune system by stimulating white blood cells. This is key because after an intense bout of exercise, your immune system is weakened for about 4 to 5 hours, leaving you susceptible to infection. Protein is also essential if you're trying to lose weight. The nutrient takes longer to digest than carbohydrates, so you feel fuller longer. And it helps keep blood-sugar levels steady, so you don't get ravenously hungry and feel the need to overeat.

For all these reasons, runners' protein needs are higher than the average person's. Every day, runners need at least 0.5 to 0.8 gram of protein per pound of weight. For a 150-pound person, that's 75 grams. Ideally, you should spread your intake throughout the day—eating some at each meal and snack—to get the most health-boosting benefits. This won't be hard to do, given the large number of protein-packed meals and snacks you'll find throughout the cookbook. (For a quick rundown of recipes that provide high amounts of protein, see the Recovery Recipes in the Special Recipe Lists on pages 257 to 258.)

While many of our protein-rich meals contain meat or chicken, plenty do not. Some feature fish or other seafood, others contain dairy or eggs, while still others are totally vegan—containing no animal products—and instead incorporate beans, lentils, tofu, nuts, and seeds. Check the Vegetarian and Vegan recipes in the Special Recipe Lists on pages 261 to 263 if you're particularly interested in these recipes. On the following pages, you'll find the best sources of protein for all runners, regardless of tastes or dietary needs.

best protein sources for runners

Vegetarian Picks
MEAT-FREE PROTEIN THAT ALL RUNNERS CAN ENJOY

Low-fat dairy
Rich in protein, calcium, and vitamin D, it provides the perfect trifecta of bone-strengthening nutrients.

Try it Immune-Boosting Raspberry-Almond Smoothie, page 60

Eggs
One egg provides 6 grams of protein. Don't toss out the yolk—it contains vital nutrients that protect your eyes and promote brain health.

Try it Egg and Bean Burrito with Avocado and Yogurt-Lime Sauce, page 34

Beans and lentils
Most varieties contain between 6 and 10 grams of protein per half cup. They're also a good source of energizing iron.

Try it Dal with Cauliflower, Eggplant, and Zucchini, page 216

Tofu
A ½-cup serving contains just 88 calories and 10 grams of protein. It's rich in heart-protective compounds called isoflavones.

Try it Brown Rice Salad with Curried Tofu, page 210

Nuts and seeds
They're a good source of heart-healthy unsaturated fats and fiber. One ounce of most nuts and seeds contains 3 to 7 grams of protein

Try it Pumpkin-Cherry Trail Mix, page 48

Meat and Poultry Picks
LEAN CHOICES OFFER PROTEIN MINUS THE FAT

Beef
Best buys Eye, top, and bottom round; sirloin; flank steak; 90 or 95 percent lean ground beef

Contains about 18 grams of protein per 3-ounce serving and no more than 6 grams of fat

Try it Barbecue Beef Sloppy Joes, page 167

Poultry
Best buys Skinless chicken breast and thighs; lean ground chicken or turkey

A 3-ounce thigh contains 18 grams of protein and 3 grams of fat—just 1 more gram of fat than breast meat. Stick with ground poultry that's 93 percent lean or higher.

Try it Southern Unfried Chicken, page 178

Pork
Best buys Pork tenderloin; boneless pork loin chops; ham and Canadian bacon

The tenderloin and chops contain 3 grams of fat and 18 grams of protein per 3 ounces, making them nearly as lean as chicken breast. Ham and Canadian bacon are leaner alternatives to traditional bacon.

Try it Mediterranean Pizza with Smoked Ham, page 125

Seafood Picks
ECO-FRIENDLY FISH THAT ALSO PACK A NUTRITIONAL PUNCH

GO-TO CHOICES

Salmon

It's rich in inflammation-reducing omega-3s. Choose wild Alaskan when possible for the least contamination and the healthiest fat ratio.

Try it Grilled Salmon with Lentil Tabbouleh, page 188

Halibut

It has a mild flavor and meaty texture. Pacific halibut from Alaska, Washington, and Oregon fisheries are the most sustainable. Avoid Atlantic halibut, which has been overfished.

Try it Pacific Halibut with Kiwi Salsa, page 198

Shrimp

With only 84 calories and a single gram of fat in 3 ounces, shrimp is very waistline friendly. US wild and farm-raised shrimp are the most sustainable choices.

Try it Garlic Shrimp with White Beans and Tomatoes, page 200

NEWBIES

Arctic char

It has a pink hue like salmon but a milder taste. Most char is farm-raised in an eco-friendly way.

Try it Maple-Glazed Arctic Char, page 196

Barramundi

Native to Australia, it's now farmed in the United States. It has a buttery, sweet flavor. Five ounces provide 27 grams of protein.

Try it Barramundi in Saffron Broth, page 194

Sablefish

Also called black cod, it's sweet with pearly white meat and contains about 30 percent more omega-3s than wild salmon.

Try it Sablefish with Pomegranate Syrup, page 197

OVERLOOKED STARS

Sardines

They contain eight times more omega-3s than canned light tuna and are a good source of vitamin D.

Try it Penne with Sardines, Prosciutto, and Cherry Tomatoes, page 151

Anchovies

Tiny in size, these fish provide big flavor and selenium, an antioxidant that may ease postexercise oxidative stress.

Try it Anchovy and Olive Pizza, page 128

Mussels

Inexpensive mussels are full of iron, a mineral needed to maintain endurance. They're farmed using eco-sound methods, with little toxin risk.

Try it Coconut-Lime Mussels, page 206

Runner's World *thanks these writers for their contributions to the introduction:*

Liz Applegate, PhD
   "Eat a Rainbow of Produce Every Day"

Matthew Kadey, MS, RD
   "Chase the Rainbow"
   "Bread and Pasta Buying Guide"
   "Best Protein Sources for Runners: Seafood Picks"
   "Best Protein Sources for Runners: Meat and Poultry Picks"

Sally Wadyka
   "Choose the Right Carbohydrates"
   "Bread and Pasta Buying Guide"

Ashley Gartland
   "Kernels of Health"
   "Liquid Gold"

Leslie Goldman
   "Get the Right Fats"

Sarah Lorge Butler
   "Meet Your Protein Needs"

Christopher Percy Collier
   "Meet Your Protein Needs"

Jessica Girdwain
   "Best Protein Sources for Runners: Vegetarian Picks"

GUIDE TO THE RECIPE KEY

At the top of each recipe, you'll find our color-coded Recipe Key. This key lets you know if the recipe meets certain training goals or dietary needs. The definitions below explain the key in detail.

PRERUN

Recipes marked Prerun supply the nutrients needed to fuel a run and can be eaten about 2 hours before a workout. The majority of calories in these recipes come from carbohydrates—your body's preferred source of energy—with no more than 30 percent of calories coming from fat. These recipes also contain fewer than 20 grams of protein and about 5 grams of fiber or fewer per serving. Fat, protein, and fiber slow digestion and can cause an upset stomach if consumed too close to running. There are many other recipes in the cookbook not marked Prerun because they may fall slightly out of these guidelines; some runners may have no problem eating these meals before a run. Because every runner has different tolerances, you should experiment to see what works for you. Remember to try any new foods long before an important race to ensure it won't upset your stomach.

RECOVERY

Recipes marked Recovery are high in protein to repair muscle tissue and provide some carbohydrates to restock your energy stores postrun. In general, optimal Recovery meals contain carbohydrates and protein in a ratio between 2:1 and 3:1, with at least 15 grams of protein. Some recipes labeled Recovery may contain slightly fewer or more carbohydrates than the suggested ratio. Regardless of the amount of carbohydrate a recipe contains, meals can also earn the Recovery label if they provide 15 to 25 grams of protein or more per serving. Fat and fiber content were not taken into consideration, since they do not significantly affect recovery.

FAST

Recipes categorized as Fast can be prepared in 30 minutes or less.

VEGETARIAN

Recipes marked Vegetarian contain no meat, poultry, or fish. They may contain eggs, dairy, and honey.

VEGAN

Recipes categorized as Vegan contain no animal products at all. These dishes are all vegetarian but additionally exclude eggs, dairy, and honey.

This category is provided for runners who may be trying to lose weight or maintain a healthy weight. These recipes contain 400 calories or fewer per serving—or 20 percent of your total daily calorie needs based on a 2,000-calorie daily diet.

Recipes marked "Gluten-Free" contain no gluten, a protein found in wheat, barley, and rye. Many of these recipes use naturally gluten-free products, including chicken, beef, and vegetable broths; gluten-free grains, such as corn, rice, quinoa, and oats; and spices or spice blends, such as curry, jerk seasoning, and poultry seasoning. However, because even naturally gluten-free products can sometimes be contaminated with trace amounts of gluten, it's key that runners who have an extreme sensitivity check product labels. Bob's Red Mill offers an extensive line of grains and flours certified gluten-free, while broths made by Pacific Natural Foods, Imagine Foods, and Kitchen Basics are gluten-free. Bottled and jarred condiments (such as soy sauce) that typically contain gluten are not used in the "Gluten-Free" recipes. However, many of these products are available in gluten-free versions and can be substituted for the traditional product.

A NOTE ABOUT SALT AND SODIUM LEVELS

Unless otherwise noted, whenever salt is called for in the ingredient list, we assume you'll use table salt. However, you can feel free to use kosher salt, sea salt, or any other kind of salt you prefer. Keep in mind that different salts have different textures and that using a finer or coarser grain salt may alter the "saltiness" of the recipe. No matter what kind of salt you use, it's best to start with a smaller amount, taste the dish, and add more if needed to suit your taste. When a recipe calls to "add salt to taste," we factored in ¼ teaspoon of added salt to the sodium analysis in the nutrition data for that recipe.

When selecting and testing recipes for the book, we made great efforts to ensure that the recipes contain a healthy amount of sodium. The dietary guidelines set by the Food and Drug Administration recommend that the general population consume no more than 2,300 milligrams (mg) of sodium a day—or about 1 teaspoon of table salt. While a few recipes in the book contain about 1,000 mg of sodium (or slightly less than half your recommended daily allowance) per serving, the vast majority of dishes fall well below that level.

In general, sodium intake is not a major concern for runners, given the amount of salt we lose through sweat on a regular basis—particularly during the hot summer months. In fact, replacing sodium is key to maintaining proper electrolyte levels. However, if you are concerned about salt or watching your salt intake, it's best to save the higher sodium recipes for days you do a particularly long or sweaty run. And runners with high blood pressure or a family history of high blood pressure should always follow their doctor's recommendations about how much sodium to have safely per day.

Breakfast

hearty whole grain muffins

Recipe by Liz Applegate, PhD

makes 12 muffins

total time: 35 minutes

It's nearly impossible to resist a freshly baked muffin. And luckily, runners don't have to. As long as they're made with whole grains (like this recipe by Runner's World's *"Fridge Wisdom" columnist Liz Applegate), muffins can offer a quick and convenient source of complex carbs, perfect for a prerun snack. After the muffins cool slightly, slice one in half and spread with a little fruit jam for more carbs or almond butter for a dose of healthy fats.*

---

1 cup whole wheat flour

½ cup oat flour

¼ cup oat bran

¼ cup ground flaxseed

1 teaspoon salt

⅓ cup packed brown sugar

2 teaspoons baking powder

½ teaspoon baking soda

2 eggs

1 cup low-fat milk, soy milk, or kefir

⅓ cup unsweetened applesauce

½ cup chopped nuts, such as walnuts, almonds, or pecans

½ cup dried or fresh fruit, such as raisins, cherries, cranberries, blueberries, or apples

Preheat the oven to 425°F. Spray a 12-cup muffin pan with cooking spray or fill with paper liners.

In a large bowl, combine the wheat flour, oat flour, oat bran, flaxseed, salt, brown sugar, baking powder, and baking soda. Mix well.

In another bowl, lightly beat the eggs. Add the milk, soy milk, or kefir and applesauce. Stir until combined. Add to the dry ingredients. Stir until just combined. Gently stir in the nuts and fruit.

Pour the batter in the muffin pan, filling each muffin cup three-quarters full. Bake for 18 to 22 minutes, or until the muffin tops are golden brown.

NUTRITION PER MUFFIN: 163 calories, 25 g carbs, 3 g fiber, 5 g protein, 6 g total fat, 1 g saturated fat, 337 mg sodium

hummingbird muffins

Recipe by Gesine Bullock-Prado

makes 15 to 18 muffins

total time: 40 minutes

Hummingbird cake is a classic Southern layer cake made with pineapple and pecans and smothered in cream cheese frosting. Runner's World *contributing pastry chef Gesine Bullock-Prado reinvented the recipe, turning the indulgent dessert into healthy—but still incredibly delicious— muffins. Her version forgoes the frosting and keeps the muffins plenty moist by using applesauce and ripe banana instead of a lot of oil or butter. Enjoy these sweet muffins as an energizing prerun breakfast.*

BATTER

- 1 cup turbinado or granulated sugar
- ⅓ cup honey
- 2 large eggs
- ¼ cup canola oil
- ½ cup unsweetened applesauce
- ½ cup crushed, drained pineapple (from an 8-ounce can)
- 2 large very ripe bananas (about 1 cup), mashed with a fork
- 1 teaspoon vanilla extract
- 1½ cups all-purpose flour
- 1 teaspoon salt
- 1 teaspoon baking powder
- ½ teaspoon baking soda
- ½ teaspoon ground cinnamon
- 2 scoops (about 2 ounces) vanilla whey protein powder
- ½ cup very finely chopped pecans

TOPPING

- ½ cup steel cut oats (not quick-cooking oats)
- ¼ cup finely chopped pecans
- 1 tablespoon butter, melted
- 3 tablespoons packed brown sugar
- Pinch of salt
- 1 tablespoon all-purpose flour

TO MAKE THE BATTER: Preheat the oven to 350°F. Spray 2 (12-cup) muffin pans with cooking spray or fill with paper liners.

In a large glass bowl, combine the sugar and honey. Microwave on medium power for 45 seconds to 1 minute. Remove the bowl and stir until combined. When slightly cooled, whisk in the eggs, one at a time, until well combined.

Add the oil and applesauce. Whisk until combined. Add the pineapple, bananas, and vanilla extract. Whisk until smooth.

In a large mixing bowl, whisk together the flour, salt, baking powder, baking soda, cinnamon, protein powder, and pecans. Add to the wet mixture and stir until the batter is well combined.

TO MAKE THE TOPPING: In a bowl, combine the oats, pecans, butter, brown sugar, salt, and flour. Mix until well combined.

Pour the batter in the muffin pans, filling each muffin cup three-quarters full. Sprinkle a light layer of topping over each muffin. Bake for 15 to 20 minutes, or until a toothpick comes out clean.

NUTRITION PER MUFFIN (BASED ON 15 MUFFINS): 275 calories, 43 g carbs, 2 g fiber, 6 g protein, 10 g total fat, 2 g saturated fat, 261 mg sodium

fresh fruit scones

Recipe by the Rodale Test Kitchen

makes 8 scones

total time: 1 hour 10 minutes

While some scones taste more like supersweet cake, these contain just a small amount of added sugar and get a boost of natural sweetness from the fresh fruit (you can use whatever fruit is in season). Adding some whole wheat flour provides long-lasting energy, while the all-purpose flour helps the scones retain their tender texture. The result is a satisfying treat with plenty of nutritional merit. Enjoy one before a run or as an afternoon snack along with a cup of coffee or tea.

- 1¾ cups all-purpose flour
- ½ cup whole wheat flour
- ½ cup sugar
- 1½ tablespoons baking powder
- ¾ teaspoon baking soda
- 6 tablespoons cold unsalted butter, cut into pieces
- ¾ to 1 cup buttermilk
- 1 teaspoon vanilla extract
- 1 cup fresh fruit, such as diced peaches, whole blueberries, chopped cherries, or diced mango

Preheat the oven to 350°F. Line the bottom of a 9"-round cake pan with parchment paper or coat the bottom with cooking spray.

In a large bowl, combine the all-purpose flour, whole wheat flour, sugar, baking powder, and baking soda. Cut in the butter using a pastry blender, fork, or two butter knives (moving the knives in the opposite direction), until the butter pieces are pea-size and coated with flour. (This creates a flakier scone.)

In a small bowl, combine ¾ cup of the buttermilk and the vanilla extract. Pour it into the dry ingredients. Stir until combined. If the mixture seems dry, add more buttermilk. Add the fruit and mix until combined.

Transfer the dough to the prepared cake pan and gently pat it into the pan. Using a butter knife, gently score the top of the batter into 8 pieces (like a pie), without cutting all the way through. Bake for 35 to 40 minutes, or until the scones are golden brown. Let them cool for about 15 minutes, then cut into 8 pieces.

NUTRITION PER SCONE: 277 calories, 44 g carbs, 2 g fiber, 5 g protein, 9 g total fat, 6 g saturated fat, 454 mg sodium

awesome granola

Recipe by Liz Applegate, PhD

**makes 10 servings
(½ cup each)**

total time: 40 minutes

The recipe name says it all—you can't beat this granola. Made with whole grains, it provides more disease-fighting antioxidants than cereals made with refined versions. While many store-bought granolas contain a lot of added oil (which significantly ups the calorie and fat content), this recipe uses just a small amount of canola oil, keeping the nutrition stats in check. Store the granola in an airtight container. Enjoy it on top of yogurt or oatmeal or by the handful for a quick snack.

**3 cups old-fashioned
rolled oats**

½ cup wheat germ

⅓ cup slivered almonds

**½ teaspoon ground
cinnamon**

⅓ cup buckwheat honey

¼ cup canola oil

⅓ cup raisins

⅓ cup dried cranberries

Preheat the oven to 300°F. Line a shallow baking pan with foil.

In a bowl, combine the oats, wheat germ, almonds, and cinnamon.

In a small saucepan, combine the honey and oil. Heat over medium heat until small bubbles appear around the sides of the pan. Pour over the oat mixture and toss until well combined.

Spread the granola evenly in the pan. Bake for 25 to 30 minutes, stirring every 10 minutes, or until the granola turns golden brown.

Remove from the oven and stir in the raisins and cranberries. Allow the granola to cool before storing.

NUTRITION PER SERVING: 259 calories, 37 g carbs, 4 g fiber, 7 g protein, 10 g total fat, 1 g saturated fat, 2 mg sodium

creamy cocoa oatmeal

Recipe by Matthew Kadey, MS, RD

makes 6 servings

total time: 35 minutes

Aside from providing energizing carbohydrates to fuel your run, this stick-to-your-ribs oatmeal is loaded with heart-protecting nutrients. Steel cut oats contain a type of soluble fiber called beta-glucan, which can help slash LDL (so-called "bad cholesterol" levels). Research shows that antioxidants found in cocoa help relax blood vessels, ease blood pressure, and improve circulation. Flaxseed is rich in omega-3s and can reduce inflammation in arteries. Serve the oatmeal topped with maple syrup and blueberries, or any fresh fruit.

- 1½ cups steel cut oats
- 2 cups water
- 2 cups low-fat milk
- 2 tablespoons maple syrup
- 1 mashed banana
- 3 tablespoons ground flaxseed
- 2 tablespoons unsweetened cocoa powder
- 1 teaspoon ground cinnamon
- ¼ teaspoon ground nutmeg
- ⅓ cup finely chopped walnuts
- ⅓ cup dried tart cherries

In a large saucepan, combine the oats, water, and milk. Bring to a boil. Reduce heat to low and simmer for 15 minutes.

Stir in the syrup, banana, flaxseed, cocoa, cinnamon, and nutmeg. Simmer for 10 minutes, stirring occasionally. Stir in the walnuts and cherries.

NUTRITION PER SERVING: 243 calories, 35 g carbs, 5 g fiber, 8 g protein, 9 g total fat, 2 g saturated fat, 44 mg sodium

savory steel cut oatmeal

Recipe by Lydia Maruniak

makes 4 servings

total time: 50 minutes

If you've never ventured beyond maple syrup, brown sugar, or other similarly sweet toppings on your oatmeal, it's time you give this savory version a try. Steel cut oats with sautéed vegetables might seem untraditional, but it's a delicious—and vitamin-packed—combination. Topping each serving with a fried egg makes this a hearty and satisfying meal you can serve any time of day.

4 tablespoons extra-virgin olive oil

1 yellow onion, cut into small dice

1 red bell pepper, cut into small dice

1 cup mushrooms (try cremini), cut into small dice

2 cloves garlic, minced

1 tablespoon balsamic vinegar

1½ cups steel cut oats

6 cups low-sodium vegetable broth

¾ cup frozen corn kernels

Salt and ground black pepper

4 eggs

5 to 6 fresh basil leaves, torn into pieces

Hot sauce (optional)

Heat 3 tablespoons of the oil in a medium pot over medium heat. Add the onion, bell pepper, and mushrooms. Cook for 10 minutes, stirring frequently, or until tender.

Add the garlic and cook for 30 seconds. Add the vinegar and deglaze the pan, scraping up any bits of vegetables that may have stuck to the bottom.

Add the oats and broth. Raise the heat to high and bring to a boil. Reduce the heat to low and simmer for 25 minutes, stirring occasionally, until the oats are cooked through.

Stir in the frozen corn and cook until heated through. Season to taste with salt and pepper.

In a large nonstick skillet, heat the remaining 1 tablespoon oil over medium heat. Add the eggs and cook to desired doneness.

Spoon the oatmeal into 4 bowls. Top each bowl with a cooked egg, basil leaves, and hot sauce, if using.

NUTRITION PER SERVING: 398 calories, 38 g carbs, 6 g fiber, 12 g protein, 21 g total fat, 4 g saturated fat, 470 mg sodium

spiced breakfast quinoa

Recipe by Melissa Lasher

makes 2 servings

total time: 25 minutes

Try swapping your oatmeal for a new hot cereal. Quinoa is a gluten-free powerhouse grain that is delicious for breakfast. One cooked cup packs 39 grams of carbs, 8 grams of protein, 5 grams of fiber, and 15 percent of your daily need for iron. Vitamin C, found in the apple, improves the body's ability to absorb this mineral. Not getting enough iron can cause fatigue and impair breathing, two symptoms that won't help your race times. Have a cup of this hot cereal for easily digestible fuel about an hour before your run, or sit down to a larger serving postrun and pair it with a glass of low-fat milk for extra recovery-friendly protein.

- ⅔ **cup quinoa**
- 1½ **cups water**
- ¼ **teaspoon ground cinnamon**
- ¼ **teaspoon ground cardamom**
- 1 **small apple, chopped**
- 2 **tablespoons dried cranberries**
- 1 **heaping tablespoon chopped walnuts**

Rinse the quinoa in a mesh sieve for 1 minute. In a saucepan over medium heat, combine the quinoa and water. Bring to a simmer, cover, reduce the heat to low, and cook for 15 minutes.

Add the cinnamon, cardamom, and apple. Cook for 5 minutes. Add the cranberries and walnuts. Stir for 1 minute, or until hot.

NUTRITION PER SERVING: 311 calories, 55 g carbs, 8 g fiber, 9 g protein, 7 g total fat, 1 g saturated fat, 11 mg sodium

stick-with-you polenta

Recipe by Liz Applegate, PhD

makes 2 servings

total time: 10 minutes

When you come back home ravenous after a long run and need to eat immediately, this is the recipe to make. Ready in just 10 minutes, it's loaded with carbohydrates to restock your energy stores and protein for muscle repair. Plus, the dried blueberries and almonds provide a health-boosting antioxidant punch.

2½ cups fat-free milk

½ cup instant polenta

¼ cup dried blueberries

¼ cup chopped almonds

2 tablespoons honey

Ground cinnamon

Pour 2 cups of the milk into a medium saucepan and bring to a boil. Whisk in the polenta, stirring for 5 minutes, or until thick.

Stir in the blueberries, almonds, and honey. Sprinkle with cinnamon to taste. Divide the polenta between 2 bowls and top each with ¼ cup of the remaining milk.

NUTRITION PER SERVING: 516 calories, 100 g carbs, 6 g fiber, 18 g protein, 7 g total fat, 1 g saturated fat, 104 mg sodium

multigrain pancakes

Recipe by Pam Anderson

makes 16 pancakes
(two 4" pancakes per serving)

total time: 35 minutes

Of all the foods that runners dream about during their weekend long runs, pancakes have to top the list. They provide plenty of carbohydrates, are fluffy yet filling, and can be personalized in a thousand delicious ways. This ultimate pancake recipe uses a mix of all-purpose flour (to make the pancakes fluffy) and whole grain flours (for added fiber, vitamins, and minerals). If you don't have all three whole grains, pick one and use the following ratios: 1:2 whole wheat to white; 1:1 oats or cornmeal to white. Simply drizzle the pancakes with maple syrup or try one of the 50—yes, 50—topping combinations suggested on pages 28 and 29. To make these pancakes the ultimate recovery meal, choose a higher protein topping (like Greek yogurt or peanut butter) or pair the stack with a glass of milk.

---

1 cup all-purpose flour

⅓ cup cornmeal

⅓ cup whole wheat flour

⅓ cup old-fashioned rolled oats

4 teaspoons sugar

½ teaspoon salt

1 teaspoon baking powder

½ teaspoon baking soda

1½ cups buttermilk

½ cup low-fat milk

2 large eggs

2 tablespoons vegetable oil, plus extra for brushing the griddle

1 teaspoon vanilla extract

Heat a large nonstick skillet or griddle over low heat. In a bowl, mix the all-purpose flour, cornmeal, whole wheat flour, oats, sugar, salt, baking powder, and baking soda.

Pour the buttermilk and milk into a 2-cup measuring cup and microwave on high for 30 seconds. Transfer to a bowl and whisk in the eggs, oil, and vanilla extract. Pour into the dry ingredients and whisk until just combined.

Increase the heat under the skillet to medium and brush with the oil. When the oil starts to spider, pour the batter, ¼ cup at a time, into the skillet or griddle. Cook for 2 to 3 minutes, or until the pancake bottoms are golden brown and the tops start to bubble. Then flip the pancakes and cook until golden brown on the other side. Repeat with the remaining batter, brushing the skillet or griddle again with oil. Serve hot.

NUTRITION PER SERVING: 200 calories, 29 g carbs, 2 g fiber, 7 g protein, 6 g total fat, 1 g saturated fat, 445 mg sodium

Multigrain Pancakes shown with
Cinnamon Peach Topping *(page 30)*

Pancake Batter and Topping Ideas

By Caitlyn Diimig

- **SWEET SUCCESS:** Mix dates, raisins, and cinnamon into the batter.

- **STOMACH SOOTHER:** Mix fresh apricot and fresh ginger into the batter. Top pancakes with honey.

- **CRANBERRY OAT:** Chop old-fashioned rolled oats in a food processor. Mix with the all-purpose flour (1:1 ratio). Add the oat mixture, dried cranberries, and orange zest to the batter. Top pancakes with cooked cranberries and cinnamon.

- **ESPRESSO DELIVERY:** Substitute espresso for half of the milk. Mix cocoa powder and hazelnuts into the batter. Top pancakes with raspberries.

- **PB BOOSTER:** Use only whole wheat and all-purpose flours (1:2 ratio). Mix bananas into the batter. Top pancakes with peanut butter and apple slices.

- **QUIRKY QUINOA:** Mix cooked quinoa and all-purpose flour (1:1 ratio). Add lemon zest, cinnamon, nutmeg, and blueberries to the batter. Dust pancakes with confectioner's sugar.

- **GREEN MONSTER:** Mix chopped baby spinach leaves into the batter. Top pancakes with strawberry puree and a sprinkle of confectioner's sugar.

- **GUAC IT OUT:** Mix corn kernels into the batter. Top pancakes with guacamole.

- **AZTEC WARRIOR:** Mix ground ancho chile pepper, unsweetened cocoa powder, and chopped dark chocolate (70% cacao) into the batter.

- **FIG AND PEAR PANCAKE:** Mix figs, pears, and walnuts into the batter. Top pancakes with vanilla Greek yogurt.

- **WAKE-UP CALL:** Mix orange zest and nutmeg into the batter.

- **BIG CHIPPER:** Mix chocolate chips into the batter. Top pancakes with whipped cream.

- **BANANA NUT:** Mix chopped walnuts and banana slices into the batter.

- **TWICE-BAKED:** Mix cooked mashed potato, thyme, and shredded Cheddar cheese into the batter.

- **BERRY MEDLEY:** Top pancakes with strawberries, blueberries, blackberries, and raspberries.

- **CHOCOLATE PEANUT BUTTER:** Mix chocolate chips into the batter. Spread peanut butter on top of pancakes and add a sprinkle of confectioner's sugar.

- **LEMON ZING:** Mix lemon zest or lemon juice and poppy seeds into the batter.

- **'CAKESGIVING:** Mix pumpkin puree and nutmeg into the batter.

- **PANCAKE S'MORE:** Mix mini marshmallows into the batter. Top pancakes with unsweetened cocoa powder.

- **HAWAIIAN:** Cook Canadian bacon or diced ham and add to the batter. Top pancakes with diced pineapple.

- **VITAMIN C BOOSTER:** Mix fresh raspberries and lemon zest into the batter.

- **PEACHES 'N' CREAM:** Top pancakes with fresh peaches and mascarpone.

- **DOWN UNDER:** Mix banana slices into the batter. Top pancakes with Nutella.

PINEAPPLE UPSIDE-DOWN PANCAKE: Mix diced pineapple and brown sugar into the batter. Top pancakes with fresh sweet cherries.

PB&J: Top pancakes with peanut butter and strawberry preserves (or fresh strawberry puree).

PATRIOT CAKES: Top pancakes with raspberries, blueberries, and plain or vanilla yogurt.

CAFÉ HOTCAKE: Substitute chai tea latte concentrate for the milk and mix pumpkin puree into the batter.

TROPICAL TREAT: Mix banana slices into the batter. Top pancakes with fresh-cut mango, papaya, and pureed pineapple.

CHERRY COCOA: Top pancakes with fresh cherries and a sprinkle of unsweetened cocoa powder.

CARAMEL APPLE: Mix diced apples into the batter. Top pancakes with caramel drizzle.

ISLAND STYLE: Mix unsweetened coconut flakes and lime zest into the batter. Top pancakes with chopped macadamia nuts.

FIESTA 'CAKES: Mix pureed black beans into the batter. Top pancakes with sour cream, chives, and salsa.

CHRISTMAS 'CAKES: Mix peppermint extract into the batter. Top pancakes with unsweetened cocoa powder.

POM-CAKES: Top pancakes with pomegranate syrup and finely chopped mint leaves.

CITRUS CRAZE: Substitute orange juice for the milk and mix lemon zest into the batter. Top pancakes with mandarin oranges.

CARROT PANCAKES: Mix shredded carrot, fresh ginger, and diced apricot into the batter.

SWEET SOUTHERNER: Mix sweet potato puree, a splash of bourbon, chopped pecans, and brown sugar into the batter.

CRUNCHY CAKES: Mix cinnamon and granola into the batter. Top pancakes with plain Greek yogurt, honey, and more granola.

STRAWBERRY RHUBARB: Mix rhubarb into the batter. Top pancakes with pureed strawberries.

ALL-AMERICAN: Top pancakes with apple slices and vanilla ice cream.

SOY SPECIAL: Substitute soy milk for the milk, and mix silken tofu and cocoa powder into the batter. Top pancakes with blackberries.

RICOTTA PEAR: Mix diced pears into the batter. Top pancakes with ricotta cheese and maple syrup.

CURRY COCONUT 'CAKES: Substitute coconut milk for the milk, and mix curry powder, turmeric, fresh-cut peaches, and mango into the batter.

LUMBERJACK: Add cooked, chopped bacon to the batter. Top pancakes with maple syrup.

KEY LIME: Top pancakes with whipped cream cheese and lime zest.

GREEN DREAM: Mix finely chopped pistachios, goat cheese, and lemon zest into the batter.

MEDITERRANEAN: Mix feta cheese into the batter. Top pancakes with kalamata olives.

SPEAKEASY SPECIAL: Mix a splash of Grand Marnier and orange zest into the batter. Top pancakes with sliced almonds and honey.

BEER BATTER: Substitute a dark beer or a raspberry beer for the milk, and mix orange zest and lemon zest into the batter.

FUNKY BLUE: Mix brown sugar into the batter. Top pancakes with a caramelized onion and blue cheese spread.

cinnamon peach topping

Recipe by Matthew Kadey, MS, RD

**makes 4 servings
(¼ cup each)**

total time: 15 minutes

You can't go wrong adding this homemade topping to any number of breakfast foods, including pancakes, waffles, French toast, oatmeal, and yogurt. Since ascorbic acid (a form of vitamin C) is added to most frozen peaches, a single cup of thawed fruit provides more than double your daily need for vitamin C. This powerful antioxidant plays a key role in keeping cartilage healthy.

1 cup frozen sliced peaches

½ cup orange juice

1 teaspoon lemon zest

½ teaspoon ground cinnamon

2 teaspoons cornstarch

2 tablespoons water

2 tablespoons maple syrup

In a small saucepan over medium heat, combine the peaches, orange juice, lemon zest, and cinnamon. Simmer for 5 minutes.

In a small glass cup, combine the cornstarch and water. Stir until smooth. Add the cornstarch mixture and maple syrup to the saucepan. Reduce the heat to low and simmer for 1 to 2 minutes, or until slightly thickened.

NUTRITION PER SERVING: 64 calories, 16 g carbs, 1 g fiber, 1 g protein, 0 g total fat, 0 g saturated fat, 2 mg sodium

sweet or savory corncakes

Recipe by Pam Anderson

makes 12 corncakes
(3 corncakes per serving)

total time: 25 minutes

While corn is often dismissed as a nutrient-poor food, it's actually rich in antioxidants. To make sure the cornmeal you buy is whole grain, avoid any labeled "degerminated" and look for the words "whole corn."

- 1 can (14.75 ounces) creamed corn
- 1 cup yellow cornmeal
- ½ cup water
- 2 tablespoons extra-virgin olive oil, plus extra for brushing the griddle
- 1 large egg
- ½ cup all-purpose flour
- 1½ teaspoons baking powder

  Optional sweet toppings: Greek yogurt, honey, and maple syrup

  Optional savory toppings: Sour cream, salsa verde, fresh cilantro, and lime juice

Heat the corn in a medium saucepan over medium heat. When warm, stir in ½ cup of the cornmeal. Whisk in the water, then the oil, then the egg.

In a bowl, mix the remaining ½ cup cornmeal with the flour and baking powder. Stir in the wet ingredients until just combined.

Heat a griddle or skillet over medium heat. Brush lightly with oil. Working in batches, drop the batter in generous ¼-cup portions onto the hot griddle. Cook, turning once, for 5 minutes, or until golden brown on both sides. Serve with your preferred topping.

NUTRITION PER SERVING: 325 calories, 57 g carbs, 3 g fiber, 8 g protein, 9 g total fat, 2 g saturated fat, 950 mg sodium

double vanilla french toast

Recipe by Liz Applegate, PhD

makes 2 servings

total time: 15 minutes

With plenty of sweet vanilla flavor, this hearty, whole grain French toast is destined to become one of your weekend breakfast staples. It supplies all the nutrients needed for recovery after a long run, while satisfying that well-earned appetite.

½ cup low-fat vanilla yogurt

¼ cup maple syrup

3 large eggs

¼ cup low-fat milk

1 teaspoon vanilla extract

1 teaspoon ground cinnamon

4 slices whole grain sourdough bread

1 cup mixed berries

In a bowl, stir together the yogurt and syrup.

Heat a large nonstick skillet over medium heat. In a large mixing bowl, whisk together the eggs, milk, vanilla extract, and cinnamon. Dip a slice of bread in the egg mixture and allow it to soak up plenty of the liquid. Set the soaked bread aside and repeat with the remaining slices.

Place the bread in the skillet and cook for 3 to 5 minutes, or until browned. Flip the bread over and cook on the other side for 2 to 3 minutes, or until browned. Serve the French toast topped with the vanilla-maple yogurt and the berries.

NUTRITION PER SERVING: 686 calories, 117 g carbs, 6 g fiber, 29 g protein, 12 g total fat, 4 g saturated fat, 996 mg sodium

egg and bean burrito with avocado and yogurt-lime sauce

Recipe by Nate Appleman

makes 4 servings

total time: 25 minutes

If you're a dedicated egg white eater, it's time to switch back to the whole egg. The yolk contains the bulk of the nutrients offered by this amazing food, including half the total protein, choline (a compound vital for healthy brain function), and lutein to protect eye health. Runner's World contributing chef Nate Appleman eats this burrito for breakfast after a morning run, but you can also make it for a quick and satisfying weeknight dinner.

¼ **cup low-fat Greek yogurt**

Juice of 1 lime

1 **tablespoon extra-virgin olive oil**

1 **red onion, cut into small dice**

1 **small jalapeño chile pepper, cut into small dice (wear plastic gloves when handling)**

½ **teaspoon ground cumin**

1 **can (15 ounces) no-salt-added black beans, drained and rinsed**

4 **eggs, mixed with a fork**

⅛ **teaspoon salt**

4 **(10") whole wheat tortillas**

½ **cup shredded Monterey Jack or Cheddar cheese**

1 **avocado, sliced**

1 **cup salsa or pico de gallo**

In a small bowl, mix together the yogurt and lime juice.

In a large skillet, heat the oil over medium heat. Add the onion and chile pepper and cook, stirring frequently, for 5 minutes, or until soft.

Add the cumin and beans and stir. When the beans are hot, add the eggs and cook until fluffy, stirring with a fork. Season with the salt. Turn off the heat.

Toast the tortillas for 1 or 2 minutes in a dry pan over medium heat, or place them under the broiler until they puff. Lay out the tortillas and divide the egg-and-bean mixture evenly among them. Top with an even amount of the cheese, avocado, and yogurt mixture. Roll up and top with salsa or pico de gallo.

NUTRITION PER SERVING: 445 calories, 47 g carbs, 10 g fiber, 20 g protein, 21 g total fat, 6 g saturated fat, 960 mg sodium

mushroom and spinach crepes

Recipe by Patricia Wells

makes 2 servings

total time: 15 minutes

These ultra-thin egg crepes make a perfect light breakfast. Or pair one with a simple green salad and serve for brunch or lunch. "The egg is simply a light envelope for whatever you want to put inside," says cookbook author and runner Patricia Wells. If you don't have spinach and mushrooms on hand, any combination of vegetables, cheese, and herbs will work.

- **2 teaspoons extra-virgin olive oil**
- **6 large mushrooms, thinly sliced**
- **⅛ teaspoon salt, plus more to taste**
- **8 ounces fresh spinach**
- **3 tablespoons water**
- **Freshly grated nutmeg**
- **2 eggs, at room temperature**
- **2 teaspoons chopped mixed fresh herbs**
- **2 tablespoons freshly grated Parmesan cheese**
- **Ground black pepper**

In a large nonstick pan, heat 1 teaspoon of the oil over medium heat. Add the mushrooms and salt and cook for 3 minutes. Remove mushrooms from the pan and set aside to drain.

In the same pan over medium heat, combine the spinach and 2 tablespoons of the water. Cover and cook for 2 minutes, or until wilted. Drain, chop, and season to taste with salt and nutmeg.

Crack 1 egg into a bowl and lightly beat with a fork. Add the remaining 1 tablespoon water.

Raise the heat under the same pan to medium-high and add ½ teaspoon of the oil. Add the beaten egg, tilting the pan to evenly spread. Cook for 2 minutes, or until the egg is just set, being careful not to overcook it. Remove the pan from the heat. Place half of the mushrooms, spinach, herbs, and cheese on the crepe. Fold the sides of the crepe over the filling. Season to taste with salt and pepper. Repeat with the second egg.

NUTRITION PER SERVING: 170 calories, 11 g carbs, 5 g fiber, 15 g protein, 12 g total fat, 3 g saturated fat, 569 mg sodium

more-vegetable-than-egg frittata

Recipe by Mark Bittman

makes 4 servings

total time: 35 minutes

"This recipe turns the frittata from an egg dish with incidental vegetables into a deliciously crisp pile of veggies nicely bound by creamy eggs," says Runner's World *contributing food writer Mark Bittman. "It's a blast of concentrated protein and plants."*

---

1 tablespoon extra-virgin olive oil

½ onion, sliced

Salt and ground black pepper

6 cups of any chopped or sliced raw or cooked vegetables, drained of excess moisture, if necessary

¼ cup fresh basil leaves, or 1 teaspoon chopped fresh tarragon or mint leaves (optional)

3 eggs

½ cup freshly grated Parmesan cheese

Heat the oil in a skillet over medium heat. When the oil is hot, add the onion and cook, sprinkling with salt and pepper to taste, for 3 minutes, or until it's soft. Add the vegetables, raise the heat, and cook, stirring occasionally, until they soften, anywhere from a couple of minutes for greens to 15 minutes for sliced potatoes. Adjust the heat so the vegetables brown a little without scorching. (If you're starting with precooked vegetables, add them to the onions and give a couple of good stirs before proceeding to the next step.)

When the vegetables are nearly done, reduce the heat to low and add the basil, if using. Cook, stirring occasionally, until the pan is almost dry, up to another 5 minutes for wetter ingredients like tomatoes or mushrooms.

Meanwhile, beat the eggs with salt and pepper to taste, along with the cheese. Pour over the vegetables, using a spoon if necessary to distribute them evenly. Cook, undisturbed, for 10 minutes, or until the eggs are barely set. (You can set them further by putting the pan in a 350°F oven for a few minutes or by running it under the broiler for a minute or two.) Cut into wedges and serve hot, warm, or at room temperature.

NUTRITION PER SERVING: 159 calories, 6 g carbs, 2 g fiber, 12 g protein, 10 g total fat, 3 g saturated fat, 366 mg sodium

corn tortilla with fig jam and roasted turkey

Recipe by Melissa Lasher

makes 1 serving

total time: 10 minutes

Sausage and bacon aren't the only meats you can eat at breakfast. Sliced turkey breast is an excellent source of protein and much lower in fat than bacon and sausage. Corn tortillas are rich in complex carbohydrates and fiber. Plus, they're gluten free. Sliced apple and fig jam provide an extra boost of sweetness and energizing carbohydrates.

- **2 small (6") 100% corn tortillas**
- **2 teaspoons fig jam (prepare the recipe for fig jam in the Fig and Prosciutto Sandwich, page 123, or use store-bought)**
- **¼ cup shredded sharp Cheddar cheese**
- **4 thin apple slices**
- **2 slices (2 ounces total) lean deli turkey**

Heat a toaster oven to 350°F. Dip your finger in a bowl of water and rub both sides of the tortillas with your finger to moisten them (this prevents the tortillas from drying out). Spread the jam on one side of both tortillas.

Set 1 tortilla on a foil-lined pan. Cover the tortilla with the cheese, apple slices, and turkey. Top with the other tortilla. Bake for 4 to 5 minutes, or until warm.

NUTRITION PER SERVING: 283 calories, 28 g carbs, 4 g fiber, 20 g protein, 10 g total fat, 6 g saturated fat, 639 mg sodium

breakfast pita with apricots, olives, and feta cheese

Recipe by Amy Gorin

makes 1 serving

total time: 10 minutes

If you run in the morning, breakfast is an ideal time to eat fruits and vegetables, including tomato, onion, and red bell pepper. They're rich in antioxidants that help reduce free radical damage caused by exercise. With their salty flavor, turkey bacon, feta cheese, and olive tapenade balance the natural sweetness of the apricots (and help replace sodium lost while sweating). They also provide protein and a bit of fat to help keep you fuller longer. Look for tapenade at the olive bar at most supermarkets.

- **2 pieces turkey bacon**
- **1 whole wheat pita**
- **1 tablespoon olive tapenade**
- **3 dried apricots, diced**
- **Half a small tomato, sliced**
- **A few thin slices of red onion**
- **¼ red bell pepper, thinly sliced**
- **3 tablespoons crumbled feta cheese**

Heat a large skillet over medium heat. Add the turkey bacon and cook for 5 minutes, or until crisp. Remove from the pan and set on a paper towel to drain.

Meanwhile, slice the pita in half and toast in a toaster. Spread the tapenade inside both pita halves. Fill the pita halves with the apricots, tomato, onion, and bell pepper. Add the turkey bacon and the feta cheese.

NUTRITION PER SERVING: 412 calories, 50 g carbs, 9 g fiber, 16 g protein, 17 g total fat, 7 g saturated fat, 1,118 mg sodium

cashew butter and mango chutney sandwich

Recipe by Amy Gorin

makes 1 serving

total time: 5 minutes

The cashew butter in this gourmet version of a PB&J sandwich supplies monounsaturated fat to keep you full and satisfied until lunch. (You can make your own cashew butter using the cashew variation in the recipe for Roasted Almond Butter on page 51.) Raisins pack energizing carbs, while cottage cheese is chock-full of protein and contains sodium to help rebalance your electrolyte levels after a run. Look for jarred mango chutney in the jam aisle at the supermarket.

- **1 whole grain English muffin, split open**
- **2 tablespoons cashew butter, store-bought or use the recipe on page 51**
- **2 tablespoons mango chutney**
- **1 tablespoon golden raisins**
- **¼ cup low-fat whipped cottage cheese**

Toast the English muffin. Spread the cashew butter on one half of the toasted muffin. Add the mango chutney, raisins, and cottage cheese. Top with the second half of the muffin.

NUTRITION PER SERVING: 525 calories, 74 g carbs, 3 g fiber, 19 g protein, 18 g total fat, 4 g saturated fat, 912 mg sodium

2

Snacks and Smoothies

43

coconut-almond energy bars

Recipe by David Santner

makes 20 bars

total time: 25 minutes

These hearty treats, adapted from The Bakery in New Paltz, New York, have powered runners, bikers, and climbers for 30 years. The oats, dates, and honey provide quick fuel, while the nuts and seeds offer enough fat and protein to fend off hunger for a good few hours. Enjoy one as a hearty snack whenever you need a boost of energy.

- **2 cups old-fashioned rolled oats**
- **1 cup unsweetened shredded coconut**
- **½ cup whole raw almonds**
- **½ cup whole raw cashews or peanuts**
- **½ cup sesame seeds**
- **½ cup raw sunflower seeds**
- **½ cup chopped dates or raisins**
- **1½ cups tahini (sesame seed paste) or natural peanut butter**
- **1 cup honey (you'll need an entire 16-ounce bottle)**
- **1 teaspoon vanilla extract**

Preheat the oven to 350°F. Generously coat a 10" x 15" baking sheet with cooking spray.

In a large bowl, combine the oats, coconut, almonds, cashews or peanuts, sesame seeds, sunflower seeds, and dates or raisins.

Combine the tahini or peanut butter and honey in a microwaveable bowl and heat on high for 1 minute. Add the vanilla extract and mix well. Add to the oat mixture. Stir until well combined.

Pour the mixture onto the prepared baking sheet and, with wet hands, pat into a rectangle about 1" high (your rectangle will be about 10" x 12"). Bake for 15 minutes, or until the edges of the bars turn golden brown. Do not overbake. The bars will still feel tacky in the center but will firm up as they cool.

NUTRITION PER BAR: 311 calories, 30 g carbs, 5 g fiber, 8 g protein, 20 g total fat, 5 g saturated fat, 26 mg sodium

banana-oat energy bars

Recipe by Lydia Maruniak

makes 12 bars

total time: 40 minutes
(plus cooling time)

These DIY energy bars are guaranteed to taste way better than any bar that comes in a plastic wrapper—and they're made with ingredients you can actually pronounce. They're also filling and satisfying, making them a better on-the-go choice than your typical snack food. If you don't like walnuts and dried cranberries, substitute any nuts and dried fruit.

¾ cup chopped walnuts

2 very overripe bananas

½ cup vegetable oil

1 cup unbleached cane sugar or granulated sugar

½ teaspoon vanilla extract

1½ cups old-fashioned rolled oats

¾ cup unbleached all-purpose flour (or replace up to ½ cup with whole wheat flour)

¾ teaspoon baking powder

½ teaspoon salt

½ teaspoon ground cinnamon

½ teaspoon ground nutmeg

¼ teaspoon baking soda

¾ cup dried cranberries

Preheat the oven to 350°F. Coat an 8" x 8" baking pan with cooking spray.

Spread the walnuts on an ungreased baking sheet and toast in the oven for 5 to 8 minutes, or just until fragrant.

Meanwhile, mash the bananas in a medium mixing bowl. Add the oil, sugar, and vanilla extract. Mix until smooth.

In a large mixing bowl, combine the oats, flour, baking powder, salt, cinnamon, nutmeg, and baking soda. Add the banana mixture and stir until just combined. Fold in the walnuts and cranberries, being careful not to overmix.

Pour the mixture into the prepared pan and spread evenly. Bake for 25 to 30 minutes, or until the top is browned and a toothpick inserted in the middle comes out nearly clean. Allow to cool completely before cutting.

NUTRITION PER BAR: 303 calories, 41 g carbs, 3 g fiber, 4 g protein, 15 g total fat, 2 g saturated fat, 158 mg sodium

pumpkin-cherry trail mix

Recipe by Liz Applegate, PhD

makes 10 servings
(¼ cup each)

total time: 5 minutes

Easy to make and long lasting, trail mix should be a go-to snack for every runner. In this mix, soy nuts, pumpkin seeds, and walnuts provide protein and key trace minerals (such as selenium and zinc for immune health), along with heart-healthy fats. Dried blueberries and tart cherries supply a wealth of antioxidants called anthocyanidins that studies show may stave off soreness. Make a big batch and keep some in your gym bag, office drawer, and car for quick energy whenever you need it.

- **1 cup dried blueberries**
- **1 cup chopped dried tart cherries**
- **1 cup roasted soy nuts**
- **1 cup walnut pieces**
- **⅔ cup shelled pumpkin seeds**

In a bowl, mix together the blueberries, cherries, soy nuts, walnuts, and pumpkin seeds. Store in a container with a tight-fitting lid.

NUTRITION PER SERVING: 264 calories, 25 g carbs, 7 g fiber, 8 g protein, 14 g total fat, 2 g saturated fat, 21 mg sodium

sweet or savory popcorn

Recipes by Rachel Meltzer Warren, MS, RD

makes 1 serving

total time: 5 minutes

Low in calories and high in fiber, popcorn is rich in polyphenol antioxidants that may protect your body from cell and tissue damage linked to heart disease and certain cancers. The key to keeping this whole grain snack healthy is to stick with plain varieties and lightly season it yourself. These two recipes will satisfy your salty craving or sweet tooth while keeping fat and calories in check. Keep in mind that only the cinnamon and sugar version is vegan.

cinnamon and sugar popcorn

- **2 tablespoons plain popcorn kernels**
- **1 teaspoon flaxseed oil**
- **1 teaspoon confectioner's sugar**
- **½ teaspoon ground cinnamon**
- **¼ teaspoon ground nutmeg**
- **⅛ teaspoon salt**

Place the popcorn kernels in a paper bag. Fold down the top a couple of times, leaving room in the bag for the kernels to pop. Microwave on high for 1 to 2 minutes, until the popping slows down to a couple seconds between pops. Give the bag a few shakes to encourage unpopped kernels to pop. Be careful not to burn yourself with steam when opening the bag.

Transfer the popcorn to a bowl and drizzle with the oil. Sprinkle with the sugar, cinnamon, nutmeg, and salt. Toss well to coat evenly.

NUTRITION PER SERVING: 149 calories, 23 g carbs, 4 g fiber, 3 g protein, 6 g total fat, 1 g saturated fat, 293 mg sodium

rosemary-parmesan popcorn

- **2 tablespoons plain popcorn kernels**
- **1 teaspoon extra-virgin olive oil**
- **1 teaspoon finely chopped fresh rosemary**
- **1 tablespoon freshly grated Parmesan cheese**

Place the popcorn kernels in a paper bag. Fold down the top a couple of times, leaving room in the bag for the kernels to pop. Microwave on high for 1 to 2 minutes, until the popping slows down to a couple seconds between pops. Give the bag a few shakes to encourage unpopped kernels to pop. Be careful not to burn yourself with steam when opening the bag.

Transfer the popcorn to a bowl and drizzle with the oil. Sprinkle with the rosemary and cheese. Toss well to coat evenly.

NUTRITION PER SERVING: 155 calories, 19 g carbs, 4 g fiber, 5 g protein, 7 g total fat, 1.5 g saturated fat, 79 mg sodium

spiced pecans

Recipe by Nate Appleman

**makes 20 servings (about
1 ounce or 2 tablespoons each)**

total time: 20 minutes

Like all nuts, pecans are high in fat, with about 200 calories and 20 grams of fat per ounce (about 20 pecan halves). But the heart-healthy unsaturated fat can help reduce LDL ("bad" cholesterol) and raise HDL ("good" cholesterol). They're also packed with bone-strengthening magnesium. Shelled pecans spoil fast, so if you don't plan to use them right away, store them in the refrigerator for up to 9 months or in the freezer for 2 years. These flavor-packed spiced pecans by Runner's World *contributing chef Nate Appleman make for a healthy anytime-snack that you can also serve as an appetizer.*

---

5 cups pecans

3 tablespoons soy sauce

½ teaspoon cayenne pepper

½ teaspoon crushed
coriander seeds

½ teaspoon ground
turmeric

1 teaspoon ground black
pepper

1 tablespoon packed brown
sugar

1 tablespoon extra-virgin
olive oil

Preheat the oven to 350°F. Line a baking sheet with waxed paper.

In a large bowl, combine the pecans, soy sauce, cayenne, coriander seeds, turmeric, black pepper, sugar, and oil. Mix well to evenly coat the pecans.

Spread the pecans out in an even layer on the baking sheet. Bake for 15 minutes, stirring the pecans once halfway through. Let the pecans cool, then store in an airtight container.

NUTRITION PER SERVING: 167 calories, 4 g carbs, 2 g fiber, 3 g protein, 19 g total fat, 1.5 g saturated fat, 151 mg sodium

roasted almond butter

Recipe by Liz Applegate, PhD

**makes 10 servings
(2 tablespoons each)**

total time: 35 minutes

Peanut butter may be a favorite food of runners, but there's good reason to swap it out for another nut butter once in a while. Two tablespoons of almond butter provide 10 percent of your daily need for vitamin E, a nutrient many runners fall short on. Studies show this antioxidant helps protect your lungs from damage caused by running in hot, humid, or polluted air. For the best prerun option, use this homemade spread on toast and apple slices, or add a tablespoon to a protein-rich smoothie for recovery. You can also substitute cashews in place of the almonds to make cashew butter.

**2 cups raw almonds or
cashews**

2 tablespoons honey

1 teaspoon salt

**¼ teaspoon ground nutmeg
(omit if using cashews)**

Preheat the oven to 325°F. Spread the almonds or cashews in a single layer on an ungreased baking sheet. Bake for 15 minutes, stirring once halfway through.

In a food processor, combine the roasted almonds or cashews, honey, salt, and nutmeg (only if using the almonds). Remove the feed tube cap from the lid. Process, stopping to scrape the sides often, for 15 minutes, or until creamy. Transfer the butter to a container and store in the refrigerator.

NUTRITION PER SERVING (ALMOND BUTTER): 178 calories, 9 g carbs, 3 g fiber, 6 g protein, 15 g total fat, 1 g saturated fat, 233 mg sodium

NUTRITION PER SERVING (CASHEW BUTTER): 138 calories, 10 g carbs, 1 g fiber, 4 g protein, 10 g total fat, 2 g saturated fat, 235 mg sodium

sliced apple with goat cheese and balsamic vinegar

Recipe by Gesine Bullock-Prado

makes 1 serving

total time: 5 minutes

This incredibly easy snack is a favorite of Runner's World *contributing pastry chef Gesine Bullock-Prado. The sweet-crisp apple provides the perfect counterpoint to the tart, creamy goat cheese. Compared to some cheeses made from cow's milk, such as Cheddar, fresh goat cheese is actually a lower-fat choice. If you have the time, let the cheese sit at room temperature for an hour before you eat it. Doing so brings out the full flavor.*

1 **sweet apple, such as Honeycrisp**

1 **ounce soft goat cheese**

2 **tablespoons chopped walnuts**

Balsamic vinegar

Cut the apple into 8 wedges and cut away the core. Spread the goat cheese on one side of each wedge. Pour the chopped walnuts onto a small plate and press the cheese side of the apples into the walnuts. Lightly drizzle with the vinegar.

NUTRITION PER SERVING: 298 calories, 29 g carbs, 5 g fiber, 9 g protein, 18 g total fat, 7 g saturated fat, 149 mg sodium

butternut squash hummus

Recipe by Matthew Kadey, MS, RD

makes 6 servings

total time: 10 minutes

This hummus-like spread has the same smooth and creamy texture as the traditional stuff, with a touch of added sweetness from butternut squash. Serve it with whole grain pita chips or sliced vegetables, such as cucumbers, red bell pepper, and sugar snap peas. Or spread it on sandwiches.

---

10 ounces frozen butternut squash cubes, thawed

⅓ cup tahini (sesame seed paste)

1 tablespoon orange zest

2 tablespoons extra-virgin olive oil

1 teaspoon ground cumin

½ teaspoon paprika

2 cloves garlic

Salt and ground black pepper

Put the squash in a food processor and puree until completely smooth. Add the tahini, orange zest, oil, cumin, paprika, and garlic. Blend until well combined. Season to taste with salt and pepper.

NUTRITION PER SERVING: 151 calories, 10 g carbs, 2 g fiber, 3 g protein, 12 g total fat, 1.5 g saturated fat, 114 mg sodium

corn-melon salsa

Recipe by Liz Applegate, PhD

makes 8 servings

total time: 1 hour 15 minutes
(including chilling time)

Salsa is an ideal snack choice for runners. Low in calories, it provides loads of vitamins, minerals, and antioxidants, while helping boost your fruit and vegetable intake. This refreshing summertime combination of fresh corn, cantaloupe, and red bell pepper is delicious as a prerun snack with whole grain tortilla chips, but you can also use it as a flavor-packed topping for grilled chicken or fish.

---

1 large ear corn, cooked, kernels cut off the cob, or ¾ cup frozen corn, thawed

¾ cup diced cantaloupe

½ cup diced red bell pepper

⅓ cup diced red onion

¼ cup chopped fresh cilantro

¼ teaspoon red-pepper flakes or diced jalapeño chile pepper (wear plastic gloves when handling the jalapeño)

Juice of ½ lime

Salt and ground black pepper

In a large bowl, combine the corn, cantaloupe, bell pepper, onion, cilantro, pepper flakes or chile pepper (to taste), and lime juice. Stir well. Season to taste with salt and pepper. Refrigerate for 1 hour to allow flavors to blend.

NUTRITION PER SERVING: 27 calories, 6 g carbs, 1 g fiber, 1 g protein, 0 g total fat, 0 g saturated fat, 79 mg sodium

good-for-you black forest blizzard

Recipe by Pam Anderson

makes 2 servings

total time: 5 minutes

Runner's World *contributing chef Pam Anderson likes to fuel up before a run with this healthful smoothie made with Greek yogurt and chocolate soy milk. Plain Greek yogurt has roughly twice the protein and half the sugar of plain traditional yogurt. Using a frozen banana instead of fresh helps chill the smoothie without ice and creates a creamy texture.*

- **1 heaping cup frozen dark sweet cherries**
- **1 frozen banana, cut into chunks**
- **1 cup chocolate soy milk or low-fat chocolate milk**
- **¼ cup plain low-fat Greek yogurt**
- **2 teaspoons honey or agave syrup**
- **¼ teaspoon almond extract**
- **4 Famous Chocolate Wafers or chocolate graham crackers, crumbled**

Combine the cherries, banana, soy milk or dairy milk, yogurt, honey or agave syrup, and almond extract in a blender. Process until creamy smooth. Divide between 2 glasses. Top each with a portion of the wafers or graham crackers.

NUTRITION PER SERVING: 273 calories, 53 g carbs, 4 g fiber, 7 g protein, 4 g total fat, 1 g saturated fat, 145 mg sodium

crunchy coffee-cocoa shake

Recipe by Jessica Girdwain

makes 1 serving

total time: 5 minutes

Not only does coffee taste great in smoothies, but it can speed your recovery, too. Research shows that having caffeine and carbohydrates at the same time helps your body restock muscle glycogen stores faster than having carbs alone. Natural cocoa powder—not Dutch-processed or alkalinized—provides anti-inflammatory antioxidants (and chocolatey flavor) for just a few calories. Almonds add crunchy texture and heart-healthy fats that help keep you full.

½ cup chilled coffee

½ cup fat-free milk

1 frozen banana, sliced

2 tablespoons unsalted almonds

2 teaspoons unsweetened natural cocoa powder

Combine the coffee, milk, banana, almonds, and cocoa powder in a blender. Process until nearly smooth.

NUTRITION PER SERVING: 259 calories, 38 g carbs, 6 g fiber, 10 g protein, 10 g total fat, 1 g saturated fat, 56 mg sodium

maple–pumpkin pie smoothie

Recipe by Jessica Girdwain

makes 1 serving

total time: 5 minutes

Who says you can only enjoy pumpkin in the fall? This refreshing, filling smoothie is ideal for recovery after a tough run any time of year. Pumpkin is high in fiber and beta-carotene, an antioxidant that protects eye health. Silken tofu lends a thick consistency and, along with soy milk, provides a nondairy source of protein—making them ideal choices for lactose-intolerant runners.

½ cup soy milk

⅓ cup canned pumpkin

⅓ cup silken tofu

1 tablespoon natural peanut butter

1 teaspoon maple syrup

¼ teaspoon pumpkin pie spice or ground cinnamon

Combine the soy milk, pumpkin, tofu, peanut butter, maple syrup, and pie spice or cinnamon in a blender. Process until smooth.

NUTRITION PER SERVING: 255 calories, 23 g carbs, 4 g fiber, 13 g protein, 12 g total fat, 1.5 g saturated fat, 127 mg sodium

blueberry-oatmeal smoothie

Recipe by Jessica Girdwain

makes 1 serving

total time: 5 minutes

There's more than one way to eat your oatmeal. When you don't feel like sitting down to a bowl of hot cereal (like after a tough summer run), try adding rolled oats to a smoothie instead. They provide a carb kick and hearty texture that will fill you up. Blend in blueberries for a dose of powerful antioxidants that help neutralize free radicals caused by exercise.

- **1 cup fat-free milk**
- **½ cup unsweetened frozen blueberries**
- **½ cup fat-free plain Greek yogurt**
- **¼ cup old-fashioned rolled oats**
- **1 tablespoon ground flaxseed**

Combine the milk, blueberries, yogurt, oats, and flaxseed in a blender. Process until smooth.

NUTRITION PER SERVING: 306 calories, 42 g carbs, 6 g fiber, 24 g protein, 5 g total fat, 0.5 g saturated fat, 149 mg sodium

melon-mango shake

Recipe by Elaine Magee, MPH, RD

makes 1 serving

total time: 5 minutes

Every runner should have a bag of frozen mango cubes in the freezer. It saves you the hassle of having to peel and slice fresh, yet still provides easy-to-digest carbs and loads of vitamin C. Juicy cantaloupe is also a rich source of vitamin C, with more than half your daily need in half a cup.

- **¾ cup frozen mango cubes**
- **½ cup frozen or fresh banana slices**
- **½ cup diced cantaloupe**
- **⅓ cup low-fat vanilla yogurt**
- **¼ cup vanilla soy milk (or low-fat milk plus 1 teaspoon vanilla extract)**
- **¼ cup granola**

Combine the mango, banana, cantaloupe, yogurt, and soy milk in a blender. Puree until thick and smooth. Pour into a glass and sprinkle the granola on top.

NUTRITION PER SERVING: 373 calories, 81 g carbs, 7 g fiber, 10 g protein, 4 g total fat, 1 g saturated fat, 145 mg sodium

Blueberry-Oatmeal Smoothie
(opposite page); Immune-Boosting
Raspberry-Almond Smoothie *(page 60)*;
and Spinach-Kiwi Cooler *(page 61)*

orange-pomegranate power smoothie

Recipe by Liz Applegate, PhD

makes 2 servings

total time: 5 minutes

A fresh orange gives this smoothie an irresistible sweet-tart flavor and provides fiber. Pomegranate juice is a concentrated source of inflammation-reducing antioxidants. For the most health benefits, read the ingredients label and buy those made of 100 percent pomegranate juice without any fillers. Leave out the protein powder for a less filling prerun smoothie.

1 cup low-fat yogurt

1 orange, peeled

1 cup frozen mixed berries

½ cup pomegranate juice

1 scoop soy protein powder

2 teaspoons honey

Combine the yogurt, orange, berries, pomegranate juice, protein powder, and honey in a blender. Process until smooth, making sure the protein powder is well blended.

NUTRITION PER SERVING: 288 calories, 53 g carbs, 6 g fiber, 19 g protein, 3 g total fat, 1 g saturated fat, 233 mg sodium

immune-boosting raspberry-almond smoothie

Recipe by Liz Applegate, PhD

makes 1 serving

total time: 5 minutes

Tough runs lower your body's ability to fight off infection, but kefir provides dozens of good-for-you probiotic bacteria that help protect against unwanted pathogens. Wheat germ contains zinc, while almonds are packed with vitamin E and manganese—three nutrients that are crucial for supporting healthy immune cells. The almonds add crunch, so if you prefer your smoothie entirely smooth, blend for 2 to 3 minutes, or use almond butter instead.

1 cup unsweetened frozen raspberries

1 cup low-fat plain kefir

2 tablespoons almonds or almond butter

1 tablespoon wheat germ

2 tablespoons honey

1 teaspoon finely chopped fresh ginger

Combine the raspberries, kefir, almonds or almond butter, wheat germ, honey, and ginger in a blender. Process for 2 to 3 minutes, or until entirely smooth.

NUTRITION PER SERVING: 446 calories, 68 g carbs, 12 g fiber, 18 g protein, 12 g total fat, 2 g saturated fat, 126 mg sodium

spinach-kiwi cooler

Recipe by Jessica Girdwain

makes 1 serving

total time: 5 minutes

Before an easy run—when you don't need a ton of calories—try blending up this lighter smoothie. Almond milk has nearly half the calories of low-fat milk, and spinach, which contains just 7 calories per cup, provides energizing iron (it also adds bright green color). Kiwi is rich in vitamin C, a nutrient that boosts your body's ability to absorb iron. Frozen, sweet banana chills the smoothie and offsets the slightly bitter greens.

½ cup unsweetened almond milk

1 cup fresh spinach

1 kiwi, sliced

½ frozen banana, sliced

Combine the almond milk, spinach, kiwi, and banana in a blender. Process until smooth.

NUTRITION PER SERVING: 123 calories, 26 g carbs, 5 g fiber, 2 g protein, 2 g total fat, 0 g saturated fat, 109 mg sodium

cherry-coconut recovery shake

Recipe by Matthew Kadey, MS, RD

makes 2 servings

total time: 5 minutes

Research on marathon runners has shown that drinking tart cherry juice can help reduce postrun muscle soreness. If the juice is too tart for your taste, try it in a smoothie like this one, which also uses sweeter fruits like strawberries. Coconut water—the clear liquid found inside coconuts—contains none of the fat found in coconut milk and adds a tangy, light, almondlike flavor. It also provides a dose of electrolytes, making this shake just as ideal before a run as after.

1 container (11 ounces) coconut water

1 cup tart cherry juice

1 scoop unflavored or vanilla soy protein powder

½ cup unsweetened frozen strawberries

1 frozen banana, cut into chunks

Combine the coconut water, juice, protein powder, strawberries, and banana in a blender. Process until smooth.

NUTRITION PER SERVING: 220 calories, 46 g carbs, 2 g fiber, 10 g protein, 1 g total fat, 0.5 g saturated fat, 58 mg sodium

3

Salads and Dressings

Salads as a Meal

Vegetable Side Salads

Grain and Bean Salads

Salad Dressings

spinach, bacon, and sweet potato salad

Recipe by Mark Bittman

makes 4 servings

total time: 35 minutes

This salad is glorious in color, full flavored, and really filling. The roasted sweet potatoes are the perfect counterbalance to the salty bacon—just a little of which adds big flavor while keeping the fat under control. Runner's World *contributing food writer Mark Bittman likes to eat this salad for a whole-meal lunch or serve it as part of a big blowout at dinner.*

- 2 sweet potatoes, peeled and cut into bite-size pieces
- 4 tablespoons extra-virgin olive oil
- Salt and ground black pepper
- 2 slices thick-cut bacon
- 1 red bell pepper, cored and chopped
- 1 small red onion, halved and thinly sliced
- 1 tablespoon peeled and minced fresh ginger
- 1 teaspoon ground cumin
- Juice from 1 orange
- 1 pound fresh spinach

Preheat the oven to 400°F. Put the potatoes on a baking sheet, drizzle with 2 tablespoons of the oil, and sprinkle with salt and black pepper to taste. Toss to coat. Roast, turning occasionally, for 25 minutes, or until crisp and brown on the outside and tender inside. Remove from the oven and keep on the pan until ready to use.

While the potatoes cook, place the bacon in a skillet over medium heat. Cook, turning once or twice, for 5 to 7 minutes, or until crisp. Drain on paper towels and pour off the fat, leaving darkened bits in the pan. When cool, break the bacon into pieces.

Return the pan to medium heat. Add the remaining 2 tablespoons oil. When it's hot, add the bell pepper, onion, and ginger. Cook, stirring occasionally, for 5 minutes, or until just softened. Stir in the cumin and the orange juice and turn off the heat. (The recipe can be made up to an hour or so ahead to this point. Gently warm the dressing again before proceeding.)

Put the spinach in a bowl large enough to comfortably toss the salad quickly. Add the sweet potatoes, bacon pieces, and the warm dressing. Toss to combine. Taste and adjust the seasoning.

NUTRITION PER SERVING: 262 calories, 22 g carbs, 6 g fiber, 8 g protein, 18 g total fat, 3 g saturated fat, 409 mg sodium

thai beef salad with mint

Recipe by Mark Bittman

makes 4 servings

total time: 15 minutes

"This is a superflavorful pile of greens topped by just a few slices of freshly grilled, juicy steak," says Runner's World *contributing food writer Mark Bittman. "I could eat this every day." Pair the high-protein salad with a hearty slice of crusty whole grain bread for a complete recovery meal. Or if you want to make a gluten-free version, choose a fish sauce or soy sauce that's made without gluten.*

---

12 ounces beef tenderloin or sirloin

4 cups torn Boston or romaine lettuce leaves, mesclun, or any salad greens mixture

1 cup torn fresh mint leaves

¼ cup chopped red onion

1 cucumber, peeled and diced

Juice of 2 limes

1 tablespoon nam pla (Thai fish sauce) or soy sauce

⅛ teaspoon cayenne pepper

½ teaspoon sugar

1 tablespoon water

Heat a charcoal or gas grill or a broiler to medium-high with the rack about 4" from the heat source. Grill or broil the beef for 5 to 10 minutes, or until medium-rare. Set it aside to cool.

In a medium bowl, toss the lettuce with the mint, onion, and cucumber. In a small bowl, combine the lime juice, fish sauce or soy sauce, cayenne, sugar, and water. The mixture will be thin. Toss the greens with this dressing, then transfer the greens to a platter, reserving the dressing left in the bowl.

Thinly slice the beef, reserving its juice. Combine the juice with the remaining dressing. Lay the slices of beef over the salad and drizzle the dressing over all.

NUTRITION PER SERVING: 170 calories, 8 g carbs, 3 g fiber, 21 g protein, 6 g total fat, 2 g saturated fat, 407 mg sodium

chicken salad with peas, feta, and mint

Recipe by Patricia Wells

makes 4 servings

total time: 15 minutes

A runner for more than 40 years, cookbook author Patricia Wells tosses together this refreshing, light lunch after a cool spring run. "The sweet, crunchy peas, tangy feta, and fresh mint are a perfect play of color, texture, and flavors," says Wells, who teaches French cooking in her adoptive homes of Paris and Provence. Peas are an excellent source of vitamin C. One cup provides nearly 100 percent of your daily need for the antioxidant. Pair it with a slice of hearty bread for a complete recovery meal.

DRESSING

- 2 tablespoons lemon juice
- ½ teaspoon salt
- 1 cup light cream or half-and-half
- ⅓ cup finely minced fresh chives

SALAD

- 1 cup shelled peas
- 3 small scallions, thinly sliced
- 3 ounces feta cheese, crumbled
- ¼ cup fresh mint leaves, chiffonade (thin strips made by laying the leaves together, rolling like a cigar, and slicing crosswise)
- 3 cups shredded cooked chicken or turkey
- 8 ounces cherry tomatoes
- 1 avocado, thinly sliced
- 2 baby romaine heads, thickly shredded
- 4 radishes, halved and thinly sliced
- ¼ cup finely chopped chives

TO MAKE THE DRESSING: Combine the lemon juice and salt in a small jar with a lid. Shake to dissolve the salt. Add the cream and chives. Shake to blend. Taste for seasoning.

TO MAKE THE SALAD: Bring a medium saucepan of water to a boil over high heat. Prepare a medium bowl of ice water. Add the peas to the boiling water and blanch for 1 to 2 minutes, or until bright green and tender. Drain (or remove with a slotted spoon) and immediately plunge the peas into the ice water to shock them.

In a large, shallow bowl, combine the cooled peas, scallions, feta cheese, mint, chicken or turkey, tomatoes, avocado, romaine, radishes, and chives. Toss with just enough dressing to evenly coat the ingredients. (Store any remaining dressing in a covered jar in the refrigerator. Use within the week.)

NUTRITION PER SERVING: 399 calories, 15 g carbs, 6 g fiber, 40 g protein, 20 g total fat, 8.5 g saturated fat, 441 mg sodium

tuna salad with parsley dressing

Recipe by Matthew Kadey, MS, RD

makes 4 servings

total time: 15 minutes

If you avoid tuna because of its mercury content, there's good news: You can put this fish back on the menu. Some newer companies, such as American Tuna, Wild Planet, and Raincoast Trading, pack smaller albacore tuna, which means the fish have less time to accumulate mercury (brands that pack large albacore still carry high levels of this toxin). All three companies harvest fish using environmentally friendly trolling or pole-and-line caught methods. While canned skipjack (or "chunk light") tuna has always been a low-mercury option, meatier-tasting albacore contains four times more omega-3s. A 4-ounce serving of albacore also packs 32 grams of protein—as much as a similar-size chicken breast.

---

4 cups baby spinach

2 cans (5 ounces each) albacore tuna, drained

1 can (15 ounces) cannellini beans, drained and rinsed

1 avocado, diced

1 red bell pepper, sliced

1 cucumber, diced

1 orange, peeled and chopped

½ cup thinly sliced red onion

1 bunch parsley, stems removed and discarded

⅓ cup extra-virgin olive oil

Juice of ½ lemon

1 tablespoon white wine vinegar

1 clove garlic, minced

¼ teaspoon salt

In a large bowl, toss together the spinach, tuna, beans, avocado, bell pepper, cucumber, orange, and onion.

In a food processor, combine the parsley, oil, lemon juice, vinegar, garlic, and salt. Pulse until smooth. Drizzle the dressing over the tuna salad and toss to combine.

NUTRITION PER SERVING: 457 calories, 26 g carbs, 9 g fiber, 23 g protein, 31 g total fat, 4 g saturated fat, 525 mg sodium

asian noodle salad
with eggs and peanut dressing

Recipe by Matthew Kadey, MS, RD

makes 4 servings

total time: 25 minutes

This hearty and filling salad makes for an impressive-looking and colorful meal—and couldn't be easier to make. Eggs are a great source of the high-quality protein that runners need for muscle repair and growth. They also provide vitamin D, which has been linked to an improvement in exercise performance. You can use the versatile peanut dressing in stir-fries, as well.

SALAD

6 eggs

2 to 2½ ounces cellophane noodles, Chinese vermicelli, or bean thread noodles

1 head lettuce, such as butterhead, larger leaves torn

2 carrots, grated

1 red bell pepper, sliced into thin strips

1 to 2 tablespoons sesame seeds

PEANUT DRESSING

⅓ cup peanuts

3 tablespoons sesame oil

3 tablespoons rice vinegar

2 tablespoons reduced-sodium soy sauce

2 teaspoons peeled and chopped fresh ginger

2 teaspoons sugar

Juice of ½ lime

1 clove garlic

¼ teaspoon red-pepper flakes

TO MAKE THE SALAD: Place the eggs in a medium saucepan and fill with water to cover. Bring to a boil over high heat. Cover, remove from the heat, and let sit for 11 minutes to hard cook. Remove the eggs from the water with a slotted spoon and transfer to a bowl of ice water to cool for 5 minutes. When cool, peel them and slice with an egg slicer.

Meanwhile, soak the noodles in very hot tap water for 10 to 15 minutes until they are flexible and no longer hard.

Divide the lettuce among 4 bowls. Remove the noodles from the soaking water, cut into 3" pieces, and place on the lettuce. Evenly divide the carrots, bell pepper, and hard-cooked eggs among the bowls.

TO MAKE THE DRESSING: In a blender, combine the peanuts, oil, rice vinegar, soy sauce, ginger, sugar, lime juice, garlic, and pepper flakes. Blend for 1 minute, or until smooth and creamy.

Drizzle the dressing over the salad. Sprinkle with the sesame seeds to taste.

NUTRITION PER SERVING: 385 calories, 25 g carbs, 3 g fiber, 14 g protein, 26 g total fat, 5 g saturated fat, 388 mg sodium

mint potato salad

Recipe by Patricia Wells

makes 4 servings

total time: 35 minutes

Cookbook author and runner Patricia Wells likes to make this healthier version of an American classic for Fourth of July get-togethers. Potatoes are rich in potassium, a mineral that helps maintain proper fluid balance and lower blood pressure. Scallions contain sulfur compounds that fight inflammation and strengthen immunity. "I like to eat the salad as a meal on its own," says Wells, "or serve it as part of a summer buffet with grilled fish or chicken."

- 1 pound firm, yellow-fleshed potatoes, such as Yukon Gold
- ¼ cup extra-virgin olive oil
- 2 tablespoons lemon juice
- 1 tablespoon Dijon mustard
- 6 small scallions, white part only, thinly sliced
- ¼ cup jarred capers, drained
- Salt
- ¼ cup fresh mint leaves, chiffonade (thin strips made by laying the leaves together, rolling like a cigar, and slicing crosswise)

Scrub the potatoes but do not peel them. Bring 1 quart of water to a simmer in the bottom of a steamer. Place the potatoes on the steaming rack and place the rack over the simmering water. Cover and steam for 25 minutes, or just until the potatoes are fully cooked. (Alternatively, you can boil the potatoes.)

Meanwhile, in a large salad bowl, combine the oil, lemon juice, and mustard and whisk to blend. Add the scallions and capers and toss to blend. Season to taste with salt.

Once the potatoes are cooked and cool enough to handle, cut them crosswise into thin slices. Add the potatoes directly to the dressing while they are still warm (so they will absorb the dressing) and toss to thoroughly coat. Add the mint and toss again. Taste for seasoning. Serve warm.

NUTRITION PER SERVING: 226 calories, 23 g carbs, 3 g fiber, 3 g protein, 14 g total fat, 2 g saturated fat, 500 mg sodium

creamy coleslaw

Recipe by Liz Applegate, PhD

makes 12 servings

total time: 1 hour 10 minutes (includes chilling time)

Swapping out high-fat mayo and using low-fat yogurt and buttermilk slashes the fat in this creamy coleslaw while adding a bit of tang. If you have a food processor, the shredding attachment will make quick work of the cabbage and carrots.

- 1 small green cabbage, shredded
- ¼ small red cabbage, shredded
- 2 carrots, grated
- 2 ribs celery, diced
- ½ cup low-fat plain yogurt
- ½ cup buttermilk
- 2 tablespoons apple cider vinegar
- 2 teaspoons sugar
- 2 teaspoons Dijon mustard
- ¼ teaspoon celery seed
- ¼ teaspoon salt
- ⅛ teaspoon red-pepper flakes

In a large bowl, combine the green and red cabbages, carrots, and celery.

In a blender or food processor, combine the yogurt, buttermilk, vinegar, sugar, mustard, celery seed, salt, and pepper flakes. Blend or process until smooth. Pour over the vegetables. Toss well and refrigerate for at least 1 hour before serving.

NUTRITION PER SERVING: 52 calories, 10 g carbs, 3 g fiber, 2 g protein, 1 g total fat, 0 g saturated fat, 124 mg sodium

fresh market slaw

Recipe by Rachel Rubin

makes 12 servings

total time: 15 minutes

The produce in this vinegar-dressed coleslaw can be found at farmers' markets throughout the summer season. Combined with staple pantry items, it makes a wonderful crisp, fresh-tasting salad. Serve it at your next barbecue in place of high-fat, mayo-laden coleslaw.

½ **green cabbage, thinly sliced**

½ **red cabbage, thinly sliced**

1 **bunch scallions, thinly sliced**

½ **cup apple cider vinegar**

¼ **cup rice wine vinegar**

2 **tablespoons honey**

2 **tablespoons sesame oil**

2 **teaspoons salt**

1 **tablespoon mustard seeds**

2 **tablespoons toasted sesame seeds**

In a large bowl, combine the green and red cabbages and scallions.

In a small bowl, whisk together the cider and rice wine vinegars, honey, oil, salt, and mustard and sesame seeds. Pour over the cabbage and toss.

Serve immediately or let it sit at room temperature for up to 1 hour to allow the flavors to meld.

NUTRITION PER SERVING: 75 calories, 10 g carbs, 2 g fiber, 2 g protein, 3 g total fat, 0.5 g saturated fat, 284 mg sodium

watermelon and feta salad

Recipe by Patricia Wells

makes 4 servings

total time: 15 minutes

Cool down after a hot summer run with this sweet, salty, refreshing, and colorful salad by cookbook author and runner Patricia Wells. Watermelon is a good source of lycopene, an antioxidant that may lower risk of developing certain cancers, cardiovascular disease, and macular degeneration. The fruit is also water-rich, helping you rehydrate after a run. Pair the salad with a few slices of toasted French bread for a light lunch.

---

2 pounds watermelon, rind removed

1 cup feta cheese, crumbled

1 cup fresh mint leaves, chiffonade (thin strips made by laying the leaves together, rolling like a cigar, and slicing crosswise), or left whole if small

1 cup mixed baby greens

¼ teaspoon salt

1½ tablespoons lemon juice

¼ cup extra-virgin olive oil or lemon oil

Cut the watermelon into large chunks. Place an equal amount of melon on each of 4 chilled dinner plates. (Alternatively, cut the melon into 4 large circles, each 1" thick and 4½" wide, and place one circle on each plate.)

Sprinkle ¼ cup each cheese, mint, and greens on top of the watermelon.

In a jar with a lid, combine the salt and lemon juice and shake to blend. Add the oil and shake once more. Taste for seasoning, then drizzle the dressing over each salad. (The dressing will keep in the refrigerator for up to 3 days.)

NUTRITION PER SERVING: 270 calories, 21 g carbs, 2 g fiber, 7 g protein, 20 g total fat, 7 g saturated fat, 543 mg sodium

cantaloupe and cucumber salad

Recipe by Patricia Wells

makes 4 servings

total time: 15 minutes

This cool, refreshing salad is ideal for a quick meal after a late-summer run. Cantaloupe adds an irresistible color, crunch, and sweetness. One cup of the hydrating fruit provides more than 100 percent of your daily need for vitamins A and C and a good dose of potassium.

½ cup plain low-fat yogurt

2 tablespoons lemon juice

¼ teaspoon salt

1 ripe cantaloupe, cut into small wedges, rind removed

2 pounds heirloom tomatoes, cut into wedges

1 cup firm goat's milk cheese, crumbled

1 small cucumber, peeled and cut into very thin slices

2 small scallions, white part only, thinly sliced

½ cup fresh basil leaves, chiffonade (thin strips made by laying the leaves together, rolling like a cigar, and slicing crosswise)

½ cup fresh mint leaves, chiffonade

Ground black pepper

In a small jar with a lid, combine the yogurt, lemon juice, and salt. Cover and shake to blend.

In a large shallow bowl, combine the cantaloupe, tomatoes, cheese, cucumber, and scallions. Toss the salad with just enough dressing to coat the ingredients lightly and evenly. Shower with the basil and mint and season generously with black pepper.

NUTRITION PER SERVING: 278 calories, 25 g carbs, 5 g fiber, 16 g protein, 9 g total fat, 3 g saturated fat, 325 mg sodium

beets with avocado and orange

Recipe by Richard Blais

makes 6 servings

total time: 35 minutes

Top Chef *winner and marathoner Richard Blais serves this inventive salad as a side at holiday meals. A good source of fiber, beets get their red hue from betalains, antioxidants with cancer-fighting properties. Serve the salad alongside roasted turkey, chicken, or fish. Wasabi paste is not always gluten free, so runners avoiding the wheat protein should check the ingredient label.*

- 1 piece (2") black licorice
- Splash of red wine vinegar
- 2 medium to large red beets (about 1 pound)
- 4 tablespoons fruit vinegar (try raspberry)
- 1 teaspoon Dijon mustard
- 1 teaspoon wasabi paste
- ¼ cup walnut oil
- Salt and ground black pepper
- 1 orange, peeled, divided into segments, and cut into bite-size pieces
- 1 avocado, cut into medium dice
- 2 tablespoons chopped fresh basil

Put the licorice in the freezer to let it get rock hard.

Meanwhile, bring a large pot of water to a boil. Add the red wine vinegar and beets. Boil, covered, for 20 to 30 minutes, or until you can stick them with a fork and it comes out easily. When the beets are cooked, peel and chop them (while still warm) into bite-size pieces.

Whisk together the fruit vinegar, mustard, wasabi, and walnut oil. Toss the beets in the mixture and season to taste with salt and pepper. Fold in the orange, avocado, and basil.

Remove the licorice from the freezer and shave atop the salad as you would Parmesan cheese.

NUTRITION PER SERVING: 169 calories, 15 g carbs, 4 g fiber, 2 g protein, 13 g total fat, 1.5 g saturated fat, 190 mg sodium

tabbouleh

Recipe by Mark Bittman

makes 4 servings

total time: 30 minutes

This classic bulgur salad "contains as many herbs as anything else," says Runner's World contributing food writer Mark Bittman. Bulgur, a whole grain, cooks relatively quickly, in just 10 to 20 minutes. Generous portions of parsley, mint, and lemon juice add fresh-tasting flavor. "If you feel the need for some additional protein," says Bittman, "top it with a hard-boiled egg."

- ½ **cup fine-grind (#1) or medium-grind (#2) bulgur**
- 1¼ **cups boiling water**
- ⅓ **cup extra-virgin olive oil, plus more if needed**
- ¼ **cup lemon juice, plus more if needed**
- **Salt and ground black pepper**
- 1 **cup coarsely chopped parsley leaves**
- 1 **cup coarsely chopped fresh mint leaves**
- 1 **cup peas or fava beans (frozen are fine; run them under cold water to thaw)**
- 6 **radishes, chopped**
- ½ **cup chopped scallions (about 5)**
- 2 **tomatoes, chopped**
- 6 **black olives, pitted and chopped, or more to taste (optional)**

Soak the bulgur in the boiling water, adding more if necessary to cover, for 10 to 20 minutes, depending on the grind, or until tender. If any water remains when the bulgur is done, put the bulgur in a fine strainer and press down on it, or squeeze it in a cloth. Toss the bulgur with the oil and lemon juice and sprinkle with salt and pepper to taste. (You can make the bulgur up to a day in advance, then cover and refrigerate. Bring to room temperature before proceeding.)

Just before you're ready to eat, add the parsley, mint, peas or fava beans, radishes, scallions, tomatoes, and olives, if using. Toss gently, taste, and adjust the seasoning, adding more oil or lemon juice as needed.

NUTRITION PER SERVING: 280 calories, 26 g carbs, 8 g fiber, 6 g protein, 19 g total fat, 2.5 g saturated fat, 208 mg sodium

chickpea, cherry, and ginger salad

Recipe by Matthew Kadey, MS, RD

makes 4 servings

total time: 10 minutes

High in carbohydrates, fiber, protein, and iron, chickpeas should be a go-to staple for vegetarian runners. Here they're combined with tart cherries, sweet mandarin oranges, and crunchy pecans for a nutrient-packed meal with loads of flavor and texture. Tart cherries are teeming with nutrients that aid in recovery, while compounds in ginger may lessen muscle pain postexercise by decreasing inflammation.

- 2 cans (15.5 ounces each) chickpeas, drained and rinsed
- 1 can (11 ounces) mandarin oranges
- ½ red onion, diced
- 1 clove garlic, minced
- 1 tablespoon peeled and minced fresh ginger
- ⅔ cup chopped pecans
- ⅔ cup dried tart cherries
- 1 jalapeño chile pepper, minced (wear plastic gloves when handling)
- 1 cup chopped parsley
- 4 ounces feta cheese, crumbled
- 2 tablespoons apple cider vinegar
- 2 tablespoons extra-virgin olive oil
- ⅛ teaspoon salt
- ⅛ teaspoon ground black pepper

In a large bowl, combine the chickpeas, oranges, onion, garlic, ginger, pecans, cherries, chile pepper, parsley, and feta cheese. Stir to combine.

In a small bowl, whisk together the vinegar and oil. Season with the salt and pepper. Pour over the chickpea salad and mix well.

NUTRITION PER SERVING: 587 calories, 70 g carbs, 17 g fiber, 16 g protein, 28 g total fat, 6.5 g saturated fat, 953 mg sodium

caprese farro salad

Recipe by Tracy Harris

makes 4 servings

total time: 35 minutes

This recipe by Tracy Harris, author of the blog The Runner's Palate, *combines all the goodness of a traditional caprese salad—fresh mozzarella, tomatoes, and basil—with farro, a whole grain that looks similar to barley and has a plump, chewy texture and full-bodied, nutty flavor. Farro is rich in protein, fiber, and vitamins and can be substituted for any whole grain, such as brown rice, barley, or quinoa. While this dish makes for a hearty meal on its own, you can also serve it as a side.*

10 ounces farro (about 1½ cups)

4 cups water

1 teaspoon salt

8 ounces cherry tomatoes, halved

8 ounces fresh mozzarella, cubed, or 8 ounces mini mozzarella balls

½ cup fresh basil, chiffonade (thin strips made by laying the leaves together, rolling like a cigar, and slicing crosswise)

¼ cup extra-virgin olive oil

2½ tablespoons balsamic vinegar

1 teaspoon agave nectar or honey

Ground black pepper

Combine the farro with the water in a medium saucepan. Add the salt. Bring to a boil over high heat, then reduce the heat to medium-low, cover, and simmer for 30 minutes, or until the farro is tender. Drain well and place in a large bowl. Add the tomatoes, mozzarella, and basil. Toss to combine.

In a small bowl, whisk together the oil, vinegar, agave nectar or honey, and pepper to taste. Drizzle over the farro mixture and toss to coat. Serve immediately or let cool and serve at room temperature.

NUTRITION PER SERVING: 530 calories, 52 g carbs, 5 g fiber, 20 g protein, 27 g total fat, 10 g saturated fat, 662 mg sodium

greek lima bean salad

Recipe by Matthew Kadey, MS, RD

makes 4 servings

total time: 10 minutes

Many runners haven't had lima beans since they were forced to eat them as kids. And that's too bad, because these bright green beans are rich in fiber and potassium and provide 12 grams of protein per cup. And, yes, they taste good, too—as long as you prepare them right. Here they get a flavor boost from feta cheese, lemon zest, and fresh herbs. Fresh lima beans are only available a few weeks in the summer, but the frozen variety is a quick and convenient year-round choice.

---

2 cups frozen lima beans

1 red bell pepper, diced

⅓ cup sliced black olives

1 ounce feta cheese, crumbled

2 tablespoons extra-virgin olive oil

1 tablespoon lemon zest

2 tablespoons chopped fresh parsley

Salt and ground black pepper

In a large microwaveable dish, cook the lima beans in the microwave according to package directions.

Add the bell pepper, olives, feta cheese, oil, lemon zest, and parsley. Season to taste with salt and black pepper. Serve as a side dish or light lunch.

NUTRITION PER SERVING: 210 calories, 24 g carbs, 6 g fiber, 8 g protein, 10 g total fat, 2 g saturated fat, 367 mg sodium

honey dressing

Recipe by Liz Applegate, PhD

makes 6 servings

total time: 5 minutes

Compared to other sweeteners, honey has higher levels of antioxidants and is also better at helping steady blood-sugar levels. Here it adds just the right amount of sweetness to the dressing. Before pouring the honey, spray the inside of the measuring cup with oil. It will pour out of the cup without making a sticky mess.

¼ cup honey

⅓ cup red wine vinegar

2 tablespoons minced scallions

Dash of salt

Dash of ground black pepper

2 tablespoons extra-virgin olive oil

In a small bowl, whisk together the honey, vinegar, scallions, salt, and pepper. While whisking, stream in the oil and whisk until combined. Taste and adjust seasonings. Toss over any salad.

NUTRITION PER SERVING: 85 calories, 12 g carbs, 0 g fiber, 0 g protein, 5 g total fat, 0.5 g saturated fat, 27 mg sodium

mustard and cumin vinaigrette

Recipe by Melissa Lasher

makes 4 servings

total time: 5 minutes

Cumin adds subtle, earthy flavor while the Dijon mustard provides tang and lends the dressing a smooth consistency. It's delicious tossed over greens as well as in a cold grain salad or used in place of mayonnaise in potato salad.

1 teaspoon finely chopped shallot

3 tablespoons sherry vinegar or white wine vinegar

1 teaspoon Dijon mustard

½ teaspoon salt

¼ teaspoon ground cumin

¼ cup extra-virgin olive oil

Ground black pepper

In a small bowl, whisk together the shallot, vinegar, mustard, salt, and cumin. Slowly whisk in the oil and 2 grinds of black pepper, or to taste. Drizzle over any salad.

NUTRITION PER SERVING: 125 calories, 1 g carbs, 0 g fiber, 0 g protein, 14 g total fat, 2 g saturated fat, 322 mg sodium

nutty olive oil dressing

Recipe by Liz Applegate, PhD

makes 12 servings

total time: 5 minutes

Heart-healthy olive oil is always a smart choice, but runners should also give less common oil varieties, such as almond and walnut, a try. The former is an excellent source of vitamin E, providing a quarter of your daily needs in 1 tablespoon, while the latter provides anti-inflammatory omega-3 fatty acids. Together they add a light, nutty flavor to this versatile dressing.

½ **cup extra-virgin olive oil**

½ **cup balsamic vinegar**

2 **tablespoons almond oil**

2 **tablespoons walnut oil**

3 **tablespoons Dijon mustard**

½ **teaspoon red-pepper flakes**

1 **teaspoon chopped fresh parsley or ½ teaspoon dried**

Salt and black pepper

Using a whisk, blend together the olive oil, vinegar, almond oil, walnut oil, mustard, pepper flakes, and parsley. Season to taste with salt and pepper. Drizzle over any salad. The dressing will keep for 2 weeks in the refrigerator.

NUTRITION PER SERVING: 133 calories, 3 g carbs, 0 g fiber, 0 g protein, 14 g total fat, 2 g saturated fat, 141 mg sodium

blackberry dressing

Recipe by Matthew Kadey, MS, RD

makes 4 servings

total time: 5 minutes

Fruit makes a surprising and tasty addition to salad dressing. One cup of antioxidant-packed blackberries contains 8 grams of fiber and a wealth of manganese, a mineral necessary for healthy connective tissue.

½ **cup frozen blackberries, thawed**

2 **tablespoons extra-virgin olive oil**

1 **tablespoon balsamic vinegar**

1 **teaspoon honey**

Handful of fresh mint

In a blender, combine the blackberries, oil, vinegar, honey, and mint. Blend for 1 minute, or until well mixed. Drizzle over any salad.

NUTRITION PER SERVING: 81 calories, 5 g carbs, 1 g fiber, 0 g protein, 7 g total fat, 1 g saturated fat, 1 mg sodium

Honey Dressing *(page 85)*;
Mustard and Cumin Vinaigrette *(page 85)*;
Nutty Olive Oil Dressing *(opposite page)*;
and Blackberry Dressing *(opposite page)*

Soups and Stews

thai avocado soup

Recipe by Liz Applegate, PhD

makes 6 servings

total time: 2 hours 5 minutes (including chilling time)

Pair this cool, creamy and thick soup with a fresh salad for a light meal on a hot summer night. Or you can use the soup to dip sliced vegetables and fruit for a healthy snack. The soup gets its smooth and creamy texture from pureed avocados, which are rich in heart-healthy monounsaturated fat. Studies have shown that substituting avocado for other sources of fat can substantially lower artery-clogging LDL (or so-called "bad cholesterol").

---

2 ripe avocados, halved and pitted

½ English cucumber, cut into ½" slices with peel on, plus more diced cucumber for garnish

1¾ cups fat-free plain yogurt

Juice of ½ lime

3 tablespoons chopped fresh cilantro

½ teaspoon chili paste or Tabasco sauce

½ teaspoon finely chopped lemongrass (optional)

Salt

1 tablespoon chopped fresh mint leaves

Using a spoon, scoop the avocado flesh out of their skins (discard the skins). Put the avocados in a blender. Add the sliced cucumber, yogurt, lime juice, cilantro, chili paste or Tabasco, and lemongrass, if using. Blend on high for 45 seconds to 1 minute, or until very smooth. Season to taste with salt.

Transfer the blender to the refrigerator. Let the soup chill for at least 2 hours to allow the flavors to blend. Pour the soup into bowls and garnish with the diced cucumber and mint leaves.

NUTRITION PER SERVING: 142 calories, 13 g carbs, 5 g fiber, 5 g protein, 10 g total fat, 1.5 g saturated fat, 151 mg sodium

chilled zucchini soup

Recipe by Patricia Wells

makes 4 servings

**total time: 2 hours 25 minutes
(including chilling time)**

If you have more zucchini than you know what to do with in the summer, try turning it into soup. The low-calorie, water-rich vegetable is high in vitamins A, B, and C, and provides the minerals potassium and magnesium—two electrolytes that help maintain fluid balance during a sweaty workout. Enjoy this soup after a run to help you rehydrate and pair it with a high-protein side for optimal recovery. An immersion blender makes it easy to puree the soup in the pot, but transferring the soup to a regular blender works just as well.

1½ **tablespoons extra-virgin olive oil**

3 **scallions, thinly sliced**

1½ **teaspoons peeled and minced ginger**

1 **pound zucchini, diced (do not peel)**

3 **cups chicken stock**

Heat the oil in a large stockpot over medium-low heat. Add the scallions and cook for 5 minutes, stirring frequently.

Add the ginger, zucchini, and chicken stock. Raise the heat to high and bring the soup to a low boil. Reduce the heat to medium-low and simmer, covered, for 10 minutes, or until the zucchini is tender.

Remove the pot from the heat. Use an immersion blender to puree the soup in the pot, or transfer the soup to a blender, being careful not to burn yourself, and puree it in batches until smooth.

Let the soup chill in the refrigerator for at least 2 hours, or until cold, before serving.

NUTRITION PER SERVING: 115 calories, 7 g carbs, 2 g fiber, 7 g protein, 8 g total fat, 1 g saturated fat, 445 mg sodium

tomatillo gazpacho

Recipe by Pam Anderson

makes 4 servings

total time: 2 hours 30 minutes
(including chilling time)

Gazpacho, a classic Spanish summer soup, is traditionally made from red tomatoes. This version instead uses tomatillos (a small, firm, green relative of the tomato), which give this cold soup a deliciously tart flavor. Tomatillos have a tightly fitting, papery husk that surrounds the fruit. Before using, peel off the husk and wash the fruit well to remove the husk's sticky residue. If you prefer a more traditional gazpacho, simply use red tomatoes in place of the tomatillos.

- 1 pound tomatillos, husked and diced
- 2 cloves garlic
- 2 cups chicken broth
- 2 tablespoons extra-virgin olive oil
- 2 avocados, cut into ½" dice
- ½ English cucumber, cut into ½" dice
- ½ red bell pepper, cut into ½" dice
- ¼ red onion, cut into ¼" dice
- 2 tablespoons chopped fresh cilantro
- 1 tablespoon lime juice
  Salt and ground black pepper

In a large pot over medium-high heat, combine the tomatillos, garlic, and broth. Bring to a boil. Reduce the heat to medium-low and simmer for 1 minute, or until the tomatillos are cooked through.

Transfer the soup to a blender. Add the oil and puree until smooth. Transfer the soup back to the pot and allow it to cool to room temperature.

Stir in the avocados, cucumber, bell pepper, and onion. Add the cilantro and lime juice. Season to taste with salt and pepper. Refrigerate for at least 2 hours, or until chilled. Keep refrigerated until ready to serve.

NUTRITION PER SERVING: 232 calories, 16 g carbs, 8 g fiber, 5 g protein, 19 g total fat, 2.5 g saturated fat, 439 mg sodium

mango gazpacho

Recipe by Marjorie Druker

makes 6 servings

**total time: 2 hours 25 minutes
(including chilling time)**

Tropical fruits and juices give this chilled soup a just-sweet-enough flavor. They also boost the total amount of carbohydrates, helping to replenish your energy stores postrun. Sodium and potassium rebalance electrolyte levels, while the mangoes provide a healthy dose of the antioxidants beta-carotene and vitamin C. Serve this soup as a refreshing first course on a hot summer night, followed by a high-protein salad, like the recipe for Chicken Salad with Peas, Feta, and Mint (page 68).

½ **English cucumber, cut
  into ½" dice**

1 **yellow bell pepper, cut
  into ½" dice**

1 **small tomato, diced**

3 **scallions, sliced**

½ **papaya, peeled, seeded,
  and cut into ½" dice**

2 **mangoes, peeled, seeded,
  and cut into ½" dice**

¼ **cup extra-virgin olive oil**

1 **clove garlic, minced**

Juice of 2 limes

1½ **teaspoons apple cider
  vinegar, white wine
  vinegar, or rice vinegar**

½ **teaspoon salt, plus more
  if needed**

1 **tablespoon chopped
  fresh cilantro (optional)**

2 **cups guava juice**

1 **quart no-salt-added
  tomato juice**

¼ **cup plain bread crumbs**

In a large pot or bowl, combine all the ingredients and mix well. Scoop 2 cups of soup out of the pot and puree in a blender until smooth.

Return the pureed soup to the pot and stir it back into the mixture. Chill for at least 2 hours. Adjust seasoning, if necessary. You can refrigerate the soup for up to 3 days.

NUTRITION PER SERVING: 252 calories, 41 g carbs, 4 g fiber, 3 g protein, 10 g total fat, 1.5 g saturated fat, 376 mg sodium

minestrone with spring vegetables

Recipe by Pam Anderson

makes 8 servings

total time: 40 minutes

This recipe proves just how easy it is to make a delicious, homemade soup with staple ingredients that are probably already in your refrigerator and pantry, such as celery, carrots, canned beans, and canned tomatoes. Leafy escarole is rich in vitamin K and folate, while beans are an excellent source of fiber. Use whatever bite-size pasta you have on hand.

2 quarts good-quality vegetable broth

1 can (14.5 ounces) petite-diced tomatoes

2 tablespoons extra-virgin olive oil

1 large onion, cut into small dice

1 rib celery, cut into small dice

1 carrot, cut into small dice

2 teaspoons Italian seasonings

¼ teaspoon red-pepper flakes

2 cans (15 ounces each) small white beans, not drained

8 ounces frozen green peas

8 ounces escarole, coarsely chopped

1 cup ditalini pasta

Salt and ground black pepper

Put the broth and tomatoes in a microwaveable bowl. Microwave on high for 5 minutes, or until steaming.

Heat the oil in a large pot over medium-high heat. Add the onion, celery, and carrot. Cook, stirring frequently, for 5 minutes, or until tender. Add the Italian seasonings and pepper flakes. Cook for 1 minute, or until fragrant.

Add the broth mixture to the pot. Add the beans, peas, escarole, and pasta. Season to taste with salt and pepper. Cover and bring to a simmer, then reduce heat to medium-low. Continue to simmer, partially covered and stirring occasionally, for 15 minutes, or until the vegetables are soft and the pasta is tender.

NUTRITION PER SERVING: 220 calories, 41 g carbs, 10 g fiber, 10 g protein, 4 g total fat, 0.5 g saturated fat, 1,049 mg sodium

potato-leek soup

Recipe by Joanna Sayago Golub

makes 8 servings

total time: 50 minutes

Potatoes and leeks are a classic pairing, and here they create a hearty fall soup perfect for dinner on a cold night. If you've never cooked leeks before, don't be intimidated by them. They do need to be thoroughly cleaned to release the dirt and sand often trapped between their layers, but doing so is easy (see the cleaning instructions in the recipe directions). After ladling the soup into bowls, you can add a sprinkle of grated Parmesan, chopped parsley, or even a few pieces of chopped bacon. Or simply enjoy it as is, paired with a slice of whole grain bread.

- 6 **small to medium leeks**
- 3 **tablespoons extra-virgin olive oil or butter, or a combination of the two**
- 6 **unpeeled red-skinned or Yukon Gold potatoes, cut into ½" cubes**
- 2 **large carrots, cut into ¼" cubes or chunks**
- 1 **teaspoon salt**
  Ground black pepper
- 8 **cups chicken broth**

To clean the leeks, chop off most of the dark leafy greens, leaving just 1" attached to the stalk. Discard the greens. Slice the stalk in half lengthwise, stopping 1" before the root end. Cut the leek crosswise into ¼" slices, stopping 1" from the root bottom. Discard the root. Put the sliced leeks in a colander. Set the colander in a large pot and fill the pot with cold water. Wash the leeks by shaking them in the water, being sure to separate the layers to get out all the dirt and sand. Remove the colander from the pot, dump the water, and repeat the cleaning once more. Set the leeks aside.

Heat a large soup pot over medium heat. Add the oil or butter. When hot, add the leeks, potatoes, and carrots. Cook, stirring often, for 3 to 5 minutes. Add the salt and season to taste with black pepper.

Add the broth to the pot. Raise the heat to high and bring the soup to a boil. Reduce heat to low, cover the pot with a lid, and let the soup simmer for 20 minutes, or until the potatoes and carrots are tender.

NUTRITION PER SERVING: 198 calories, 36 g carbs, 5 g fiber, 7 g protein, 4 g total fat, 0.5 g saturated fat, 884 mg sodium

celeriac and potato soup

Recipe by Matthew Kadey, MS, RD

makes 6 servings

total time: 40 minutes

With its rough, bumpy skin, celeriac may be the ugly duckling of the vegetable world, but it has tender flesh that tastes like a combination of celery and parsley. What it lacks in aesthetics, celeriac (which is also called celery root) makes up for with stellar amounts of vitamin K— 80 percent of your daily need in a 1-cup serving. Vitamin K plays a key role in bone development and maintaining flexible blood vessels, both of which are important for runners. Small- to medium-size roots have the best flavor and texture.

1 celeriac

4 cups low-sodium vegetable broth

2 potatoes, peeled and cut into ¼" slices

2 leeks, sliced and washed (see washing instructions in the Potato-Leek Soup recipe on page 98)

1 clove garlic, chopped

Salt and ground black pepper

Use a sharp knife to remove the base and top of the celeriac so that the vegetable sits flat. Cut down the sides of the celeriac, slicing off about ½" of the vegetable's thick skin all around. Cut the remaining root into ¼" slices.

Heat a large pot over high heat. Add the celeriac, broth, potatoes, leeks, and garlic. Season to taste with salt and pepper. Bring to a boil. Reduce the heat to medium-low and simmer, covered, for 15 to 20 minutes, or until the vegetables are completely tender.

Use an immersion blender to puree the soup in the pot until smooth. Alternatively, transfer the soup to a blender, being careful not to burn yourself, and puree (in batches if necessary) until smooth.

NUTRITION PER SERVING: 189 calories, 40 g carbs, 7 g fiber, 6 g protein, 1 g total fat, 0 g saturated fat, 482 mg sodium

chickpea-pesto tomato soup

Recipe by Jessica Girdwain

makes 4 servings

total time: 30 minutes

Classic tomato soup gets a health and taste upgrade with this quick-and-easy recipe, thanks to the addition of chickpeas. Research shows that people who eat just half a cup of fiber-rich chickpeas a day eat less junk food and feel fuller after a meal than people who don't eat them. Tomatoes are an excellent source of the antioxidant lycopene, which studies show can protect your skin from ultraviolet rays—important for runners logging miles in the sun.

- 1 tablespoon extra-virgin olive oil
- 1 onion, diced
- 2 cloves garlic, minced
- 1 can (28 ounces) fire-roasted crushed tomatoes
- 2 cups low-sodium vegetable broth
- 1 teaspoon sugar
- ¼ teaspoon ground black pepper, plus more as needed
- 1 can (15 ounces) chickpeas, drained and rinsed
- ¼ cup basil pesto (use jarred or the recipe for pesto in Portobello and Asparagus Pasta on page 148)

Heat the oil in a large soup pot over medium heat. Add the onion and cook, stirring frequently, for 4 minutes, or until soft.

Add the garlic and cook, stirring frequently, for about 30 seconds. Add the tomatoes and broth. Raise the heat to high and bring the soup to a boil. Reduce the heat to low and simmer for 5 minutes. Add the sugar and pepper.

If you prefer a smooth texture, transfer the mixture to a blender and puree until smooth. Then transfer the soup back to the pot. If you prefer a chunky texture, skip this step.

Add the chickpeas to the pot. Cover with a lid and simmer for 10 minutes. Season to taste with pepper. Ladle the soup into bowls and top with a dollop of pesto.

NUTRITION PER SERVING: 258 calories, 38 g carbs, 7 g fiber, 8 g protein, 10 g total fat, 1.5 g saturated fat, 947 mg sodium

curried coconut-squash soup

Recipe by Jessica Girdwain

makes 4 servings

total time: 30 minutes

This rich-tasting, velvety-smooth soup gets its creaminess from light coconut milk, which has 60 percent fewer calories than the full-fat version. Curry powder contains turmeric, a spice with strong anti-inflammatory properties. Research indicates that turmeric can help keep joints healthy and protect against arthritis. Look for packages of cubed butternut squash in the produce section or in the frozen food aisle at the supermarket.

---

3 cups fresh or frozen cubed butternut squash (1" cubes)

¼ cup water

1 can (14 ounces) light coconut milk

2 cups low-sodium chicken broth

1 teaspoon curry powder

½ teaspoon salt

¼ cup low-fat plain Greek yogurt

Put the squash in a microwaveable dish. Add the water and loosely cover the dish. Steam it in the microwave on high for 5 to 10 minutes, or until the squash is soft. Let it cool in the microwave for 1 minute.

In a blender, combine the squash, coconut milk, broth, curry powder, and salt. Puree until smooth.

Transfer the soup to a pot and heat over medium heat for 10 minutes, or until gently simmering. Ladle the soup into bowls and top each with a dollop of yogurt.

NUTRITION PER SERVING: 126 calories, 14 g carbs, 2 g fiber, 5 g protein, 6 g total fat, 5 g saturated fat, 354 mg sodium

red lentil and black bean stew

Recipe by Jessica Girdwain

makes 4 servings

total time: 50 minutes

This meatless stew is thick and superfilling, thanks to the beans and lentils. Both are good sources of protein and fiber-rich carbs. The body absorbs these nutrients slowly, keeping energy levels on an even keel. Chili powder, cumin, and paprika punch up the flavor while providing a dose of anti-inflammatory antioxidants. If you can't find red lentils, any color will work.

- 1 tablespoon extra-virgin olive oil
- 1 onion, chopped
- 2 cloves garlic, minced
- ½ teaspoon chili powder
- ½ teaspoon ground cumin
- ¼ teaspoon paprika
- 4 cups low-sodium vegetable broth
- 1 tablespoon tomato paste
- ¾ cup red lentils
- 1 can (15 ounces) black beans, drained and rinsed, mashing half the beans with a fork
- Juice of 1 lime
- ¼ teaspoon salt
- ¼ teaspoon ground black pepper
- 2 tablespoons chopped fresh cilantro

Heat the oil in a large soup pot over medium heat. Add the onion and cook, stirring frequently, for 5 minutes, or until soft. Add the garlic, chili powder, cumin, and paprika and cook for 1 minute. Add the broth and tomato paste. Raise the heat to high and bring the mixture to a boil. Add the lentils. Reduce the heat to a simmer and cook for 25 minutes, or until the lentils are tender.

Add the black beans (both whole and mashed), lime juice, salt, and pepper. Cook for 5 minutes, or until heated through. Ladle into bowls and sprinkle with the cilantro.

NUTRITION PER SERVING: 248 calories, 38 g carbs, 10 g fiber, 14 g protein, 5 g total fat, 0.5 g saturated fat, 542 mg sodium

slow-cooked clam chowder

Recipe by Liz Applegate, PhD

makes 4 servings

total time: 5 hours

Clam chowder is often a high-fat disaster, but this version trims the fat down to just 4 grams per hearty serving by using fat-free evaporated milk. While this makes a thinner broth, it still has a surprisingly rich and silky mouth-feel. Don't be tempted to swap in regular fat-free milk—it's too watery to use here. Heating the soup in a slow cooker means you can be free to do other things (like go for a run) while dinner cooks.

---

1 tablespoon extra-virgin olive oil

1 onion, diced

2 ribs celery, diced

2 teaspoons minced garlic

2 cans (8 ounces each) clams

1 bottle (8 ounces) clam juice

3 potatoes (any kind), cut into bite-size cubes

1 can (12 ounces) fat-free evaporated milk

Ground black pepper

Heat the oil in a medium skillet over medium-low heat. Add the onion and celery. Cook, stirring often, for 12 minutes, or until soft and translucent. Add the garlic and cook for 1 minute. Transfer the mixture to a slow cooker.

Add the clams (with juice), clam juice, and potatoes to the slow cooker. Cover with a lid and cook on high for 2 to 3 hours or on low for 4 to 5 hours, or until the potatoes are tender.

During the last hour of cooking, when the potatoes are nearly done, add the evaporated milk. Season to taste with pepper.

NUTRITION PER SERVING: 375 calories, 65 g carbs, 4 g fiber, 21 g protein, 4 g total fat, 0.5 g saturated fat, 993 mg sodium

creamy potato-spinach soup

Recipe by Matthew Kadey, MS, RD

makes 4 servings

total time: 30 minutes

Make this quick-and-easy soup for dinner on a weeknight and pair it with a whole grain roll and salad. A half cup of cooked frozen spinach packs more than 640 percent of your daily need for bone-protecting vitamin K, nearly 230 percent of your daily need for vitamin A, and nearly 30 percent of your daily folate need. Folate, a B vitamin, helps red blood cells carry oxygen to working muscles—and not getting enough of it will make your runs seem more taxing.

- **2 teaspoons extra-virgin olive oil**
- **1 onion, chopped**
- **4 cups low-sodium vegetable broth**
- **1 box (10 ounces) frozen spinach (thawed, juices retained)**
- **1 potato, chopped**
- **1 teaspoon ground cumin**
- **Salt and ground black pepper**
- **Juice of 1 lemon**
- **½ cup low-fat plain Greek yogurt**

Heat the oil in a large pot over medium heat. Add the onion and cook, stirring frequently, for 4 minutes, or until softened.

Add the broth, spinach, potato, and cumin. Season to taste with salt and pepper. Raise the heat and bring the soup to a boil. Reduce the heat to low and simmer for 10 to 15 minutes, or until the potato is tender.

Using an immersion blender, puree the soup in the pot until smooth. Alternatively, transfer the soup to a blender, being careful not to burn yourself, and puree until smooth. Transfer back to the pot.

Add the lemon juice and yogurt. Stir until combined. Reheat if necessary.

NUTRITION PER SERVING: 107 calories, 16 g carbs, 3 g fiber, 4 g protein, 3 g total fat, 1 g saturated fat, 300 mg sodium

chicken-quinoa soup

Recipe by Matthew Kadey, MS, RD

makes 6 servings

total time: 45 minutes

Chicken-noodle soup gets a healthy upgrade with this whole grain, vegetable-packed version. The carbohydrates in quick-cooking quinoa restock your energy stores, while the amino acids in chicken help rebuild broken-down muscle tissue postrun, making this soup the ideal recovery meal.

2 teaspoons canola oil

1 onion, diced

2 carrots, sliced

1 pound boneless chicken thighs, thinly sliced

1 cup sliced mushrooms

2 ribs celery, sliced

2 cloves garlic, minced

4 cups chicken broth

1 cup water

¾ cup quinoa

2 teaspoons fresh thyme or 1 teaspoon dried

Salt and ground black pepper

Chopped fresh parsley (optional)

Hot sauce (optional)

Heat the oil in a large pot over medium heat. Add the onion and carrots. Cook, stirring frequently, for 6 minutes. Add the chicken, mushrooms, celery, and garlic. Cook, stirring frequently, for 5 minutes.

Add the broth, water, quinoa, and thyme. Season to taste with salt and pepper. Raise the heat to high and bring the soup to a boil. Reduce the heat to low and simmer for 15 minutes, or until the quinoa is tender. Ladle into bowls and top with the parsley and hot sauce, if using.

NUTRITION PER SERVING: 214 calories, 18 g carbs, 3 g fiber, 19 g protein, 7 g total fat, 1 g saturated fat, 811 mg sodium

spicy sausage and mushroom soup

Recipe by Jessica Girdwain

makes 4 servings

total time: 1 hour

Wild rice and chicken sausage provide the carb-and-protein combo that runners need after a long run, while keeping fat and calories in check. Mushrooms lend a hearty, almost meatlike texture. In fact, a study found that people who substitute mushrooms for meat consume fewer calories and feel just as satisfied as when they eat meat-heavy meals. You can make this dish in half the time by using already-cooked rice—a great way to use up leftovers. Sausage is often gluten free, but supersensitive runners should check the package to be sure.

¾ **cup wild rice**

1 **tablespoon extra-virgin olive oil**

1 **pound precooked spicy chicken sausage, sliced**

2 **packages (8 ounces each) sliced mushrooms (try cremini or white button)**

¼ **cup water**

¼ **teaspoon dried thyme**

¼ **teaspoon red-pepper flakes**

4 **cups chopped kale**

¼ **cup white wine**

6 **cups low-sodium chicken broth**

Ground black pepper

In a medium saucepan, cook the rice according to the package directions.

Meanwhile, heat the oil in a soup pot over medium-high heat. Add the sausage and cook for 5 to 6 minutes, or until brown. (If you use raw sausage, cook for 8 to 10 minutes, or until brown and cooked through.) Remove the sausage.

In the same pot, add the mushrooms and cook for 5 to 8 minutes, or until soft and browned. Add the water, scraping up the sausage bits stuck to the bottom of the pan. Add the thyme, pepper flakes, kale, and wine. Cook for 4 minutes, or until the kale is wilted. Add the broth and simmer for 15 minutes. Season to taste with pepper.

When the rice is cooked, stir it into the soup along with the sausage. Simmer for 5 minutes, or until hot.

NUTRITION PER SERVING: 425 calories, 39 g carbs, 4 g fiber, 36 g protein, 16 g total fat, 3.5 g saturated fat, 788 mg sodium

wheat berry and beef stew

Recipe by Liz Applegate, PhD

makes 4 servings

total time: 6 hours 20 minutes

Warm up on a cold winter night with this hearty stew loaded with protein, fiber, and iron—a key mineral that runners need to maintain endurance. To vary the flavor, you can swap in up to 1½ cups of stout in place of the broth. Don't use parcooked wheat berries. While they cook faster, they absorb too much liquid and will fall apart in the stew. If you can only find parcooked, add them in the last hour of cooking.

- **1 to 2 tablespoons extra-virgin olive oil**
- **¾ pound cubed beef stew meat (1 to 1½" cubes)**
- **2 tablespoons all-purpose flour**
- **Salt and ground black pepper**
- **2 ribs celery, sliced ½" thick**
- **1 leek, cleaned and sliced 1" thick**
- **1 yellow or white onion, cut into ½" dice**
- **3 carrots, chopped into ¾" pieces**
- **2 cloves garlic, minced**
- **4 cups low-sodium beef broth**
- **1 cup wheat berries**
- **1 tablespoon tomato paste**
- **1 tablespoon Worcestershire sauce**
- **1 bay leaf**
- **2 teaspoons dried thyme**
- **½ teaspoon red-pepper flakes (optional)**

Heat a large skillet over medium-high heat. Add 1 tablespoon of the oil.

Meanwhile, place the stew meat, flour, and a few dashes of salt and pepper in a large resealable plastic bag. Seal it and shake until all the meat is coated with flour. Add the meat to the hot pan and brown on all sides, in batches if necessary, for 5 minutes. (Add the second tablespoon of oil, if necessary, to prevent the meat from burning.) Transfer the beef to a plate.

Add the celery, leek, and onion to the skillet. Cook for 2 minutes, stirring constantly. Add the carrots and cook, stirring, for 3 minutes. Add the garlic and cook for 1 minute. Transfer the vegetables to a slow cooker.

Add ½ cup of the broth to the skillet and scrape up the brown bits on the bottom. Add the broth and scrapings to the slow cooker. Add the beef (and any juices that collected on the plate), wheat berries, tomato paste, Worcestershire sauce, bay leaf, thyme, pepper flakes (if using), and the remaining 3½ cups broth to the slow cooker. Cover securely with a lid and cook on low for 6 hours.

After 6 hours, stir the stew, season to taste with salt and pepper, and check for doneness. The meat, vegetables, and wheat berries should be very tender. If not, cook for another 1 to 2 hours. Remove the bay leaf before serving.

NUTRITION PER SERVING: 444 calories, 51 g carbs, 9 g fiber, 27 g protein, 15 g total fat, 5 g saturated fat, 736 mg sodium

crunchy cocoa chili

Recipe by Matthew Kadey, MS, RD

makes 6 servings

total time: 1 hour

This no-fuss vegetarian chili gets a protein boost from tofu and canned beans. Cocoa powder may seem like an unusual addition, but it adds rich, subtle flavor and plenty of polyphenol antioxidants that may blunt the effects of exercise-induced oxidative stress. Topping each serving with crushed, whole grain tortilla chips provides a satisfying crunch.

- 1 tablespoon canola oil
- 1 onion, diced
- 1 package (8 ounces) sliced mushrooms (try cremini or white button)
- 1 block (14 ounces) firm tofu, drained and cut into ½" dice
- 2 teaspoons ground cumin
- 1 teaspoon chili powder
- 1 clove garlic, minced
- Salt and ground black pepper
- 1 can (28 ounces) diced tomatoes
- 1 can (6 ounces) tomato paste
- 1 can (15 ounces) black beans, drained and rinsed
- 1 can (15 ounces) kidney beans, drained and rinsed
- 1 cup frozen corn
- 2 tablespoons unsweetened cocoa powder
- 1 cup crushed whole grain tortilla chips

Heat the oil in a medium soup pot over medium heat. Add the onion and mushrooms. Cook, stirring frequently, for 4 minutes.

Stir in the tofu, cumin, chili powder, and garlic. Season to taste with salt and pepper. Cook for 3 minutes, stirring occasionally.

Add the tomatoes, tomato paste, black beans, kidney beans, corn, and cocoa powder. Raise the heat to high and bring the mixture to a boil. Reduce the heat to medium-low and simmer for 30 minutes, stirring occasionally.

Ladle the chili into bowls and serve topped with the tortilla chips.

NUTRITION PER SERVING: 304 calories, 43 g carbs, 10 g fiber, 16 g protein, 9 g total fat, 1 g saturated fat, 862 mg sodium

bean and vegetable chili

Recipe by Mark Bittman

makes 6 servings

total time: 1 hour

This not-quite-vegetarian recipe—from Runner's World *contributing food writer Mark Bittman—features lots of vegetables and fiber-rich beans, seasoned with a small amount of meat, which lends rich flavor while keeping the fat to a minimum. Use whatever beans you like, or add lentils, which break down and add meaty texture to the chili. Serve with brown rice, crackers, tortilla chips, or whole grain bread.*

---

3 tablespoons olive oil

½ pound ground beef, pork, turkey, or chicken

Salt and ground black pepper

1 onion, chopped

1 tablespoon minced garlic

2 small eggplants, cubed

1 zucchini, chopped

2 carrots, chopped

1 cup quartered mushrooms

1 fresh or dried hot chile pepper, seeded and minced (optional), wear plastic gloves when handling

1 teaspoon ground cumin

1 teaspoon minced fresh oregano leaves or ½ teaspoon dried

1 cup peeled, seeded, and chopped tomatoes (canned is fine; don't drain)

4 cups canned kidney beans, liquid reserved

2 cups vegetable broth or more as needed, optional

Chopped fresh cilantro or scallions

Heat the oil in a large pot over medium heat. When the oil is hot, add the meat. Sprinkle with salt and pepper to taste, and cook, stirring frequently, for 10 minutes, or until well browned all over. Remove the meat from the pot and drain off all but 3 tablespoons of the fat.

Return the pot to the stove over medium-high heat. Add the onion and garlic. Stir and cook for 1 minute, or until just softened. Add the eggplants, zucchini, carrots, and mushrooms. Sprinkle with salt and pepper to taste. Cook, stirring occasionally, for 10 minutes, or until they begin to soften and become fragrant, adjusting the heat so that nothing scorches (the vegetables should start to caramelize a bit and dry out).

Stir in the chile pepper (if using), cumin, and oregano. Add the tomatoes and beans with enough of their liquid to submerge everything (use the broth or water if you don't have enough). Bring the mixture to a boil and cook, stirring occasionally and adding more liquid if necessary, for 15 minutes, or until the beans are very tender and the flavors have mellowed. Taste and adjust the seasoning. Serve garnished with cilantro or scallions.

NUTRITION PER SERVING: 313 calories, 37 g carbs, 12 g fiber, 19 g protein, 10 g total fat, 2 g saturated fat, 824 mg sodium

Sandwiches, Pizzas, and Burgers

Meat

Fish and Seafood

Vegetarian

meat and grain burgers

Recipe by Mark Bittman

makes 6 servings

total time: 40 minutes

Runner's World *contributing food writer Mark Bittman loves a good—and healthy—hamburger after a long run. By using his tip to combine ground meat with cooked whole grains, you can create a burger that's moist, flavorful, and high in fiber with less unhealthy saturated fat. If using bulgur, soak it in twice the volume of hot water for 20 to 30 minutes before draining.*

2 tablespoons vegetable oil

Salt

1 pound fresh spinach leaves

1 pound beef chuck or sirloin, boneless chicken or turkey thighs, or pork or lamb shoulder, excess fat removed; or use already ground meat

1 small onion, finely chopped

2 cloves garlic, finely chopped

Pinch of cayenne pepper

1 teaspoon ground cumin, or 1 tablespoon chili powder

¼ teaspoon salt

¼ teaspoon ground black pepper

1 egg

2 cups soaked and drained bulgur, or other cooked grains like cracked wheat, steel cut oats, or whole wheat couscous

6 whole wheat burger buns

Preheat the oven to 400°F. Grease a rimmed baking sheet or large roasting pan with the oil.

Bring a large pot of water to a boil and salt it. Fill a large bowl with ice water. Wilt the spinach in the boiling water for about 30 seconds. Drain and immediately plunge into the ice water. Drain, squeeze tightly to dry thoroughly, and coarsely chop. Put the spinach in a bowl. If you're using ground meat, add it to the spinach and skip the next paragraph.

If you're using whole pieces of meat, cut them into large chunks and put them in a food processor. Pulse several times to process until ground but not pureed, stopping the machine and scraping down the sides, if necessary. Transfer to the bowl with the spinach.

Add the onion, garlic, cayenne, and cumin or chili powder. Sprinkle with ¼ teaspoon salt and pepper, and stir. Add the egg and grains and mix until thoroughly combined using a rubber spatula or your hands. Shape into 6 burgers and put on the baking sheet or in the roasting pan. Transfer to the oven and roast for 20 to 30 minutes, or until firm and browned all over. (Carefully turn them once or twice for even cooking.) Since the burgers are pretty sturdy, they can also be cooked on a preheated grill over medium heat for 3 or 4 minutes per side.

Place the burgers in the buns and top with salsa or any of your favorite burger toppings.

NUTRITION PER SERVING: 327 calories, 38 g carbs, 8 g fiber, 24 g protein, 11 g total fat, 2 g saturated fat, 421 mg sodium

roast beef pita with cucumber-yogurt sauce

Recipe by Liz Applegate, PhD

makes 1 serving
total time: 10 minutes

Assemble this meal in the morning and bring it to work for an energizing postrun lunch at your desk. Roast beef is naturally lean and rich in easily absorbed iron. Use any remaining yogurt sauce to dip extra cucumber spears.

½ cup low-fat plain yogurt

⅓ cucumber, chopped

1 teaspoon fresh dill or a sprinkle of dried

2 tablespoons hummus

1 small (4") whole wheat pita, cut in half

3 ounces thin-sliced lean roast beef

In a small bowl, stir together the yogurt, cucumber, and dill.

Spread 1 tablespoon hummus in each pita half. Stuff each with an equal amount of the roast beef. Spoon the yogurt sauce into each pita half.

NUTRITION PER SERVING: 364 calories, 31 g carbs, 5 g fiber, 36 g protein, 11 g total fat, 4 g saturated fat, 384 mg sodium

chicken-pesto sandwich

Recipe by Matthew Kadey, MS, RD

makes 2 servings

total time: 10 minutes

Sandwiches are a great way to sneak a variety of vegetables into your diet. Swap out your standard slice of tomato for just 2 tablespoons of shredded carrot and you'll get well over 50 percent of your daily need for the antioxidant vitamin A in the form of beta-carotene. Jarred pesto is a must-have staple for runners. Keep a jar in your pantry for quick meals like this one. Or use the recipe for Basil-Mint Pesto on page 141— freeze any extra to use in future recipes.

6 ounces cooked and shredded chicken breast

1 tablespoon Basil-Mint Pesto (page 141) or jarred pesto

2 whole wheat English muffins, halved and toasted, or 4 slices whole wheat bread

¼ cup shredded carrots

1 cup mixed baby greens

In a bowl, mix together the chicken and pesto. Put half the chicken mixture on one half of each English muffin or on 2 slices of the bread. Top each with half the carrots, half the baby greens, and the second half of both English muffins or the remaining slices of bread.

NUTRITION PER SERVING: 324 calories, 30 g carbs, 6 g fiber, 34 g protein, 8 g total fat, 2 g saturated fat, 561 mg sodium

curried chicken salad sandwich with cranberries and pine nuts

Recipe by Elaine Magee, MPH, RD

makes 4 servings

total time: 15 minutes

Too often, runners skimp on calories at lunch, opting to eat a quick bite on the go or to graze on whatever energy bar or snacks might be hanging around the office. But doing so may leave you ravenous by dinner and more likely to overeat. This hearty chicken salad recipe provides whole grain carbs, filling fiber, and plenty of protein—and will provide the energy you need to get through the rest of your day.

- **3 cups shredded cooked skinless chicken breast**
- **3 tablespoons dried cranberries**
- **3 tablespoons toasted pine nuts**
- **1 cup diced apple**
- **¼ cup mayonnaise**
- **¼ cup sour cream**
- **1 tablespoon honey mustard**
- **1 teaspoon curry powder**
- **2 cups spring greens or fresh baby spinach**
- **8 slices whole wheat bread**

In a medium bowl, combine the chicken, cranberries, pine nuts, and apple. Toss together.

In a small bowl, whisk together the mayonnaise, sour cream, honey mustard, and curry until blended and smooth. Spoon it over the chicken mixture and toss to blend.

Place ½ cup of the greens on each of 4 slices of bread. Top each with 1 cup of the chicken salad. Place a slice of bread on top of each.

NUTRITION PER SERVING: 522 calories, 36 g carbs, 6 g fiber, 42 g protein, 24 g total fat, 4.5 g saturated fat, 464 mg sodium

chicken pitas with sun-dried tomato spread

Recipe by Matthew Kadey, MS, RD

makes 4 servings

total time: 35 minutes

Sun-dried tomatoes are a concentrated source of lycopene. This antioxidant has been shown to reduce your risk of certain cancers, including prostate cancer. While sun-dried tomatoes packed in oil contain more fat and calories than those packed in water, that added oil is needed to give the spread a smooth, rich consistency. Double the recipe for the tomato spread and keep the extra in a container in the refrigerator for up to 2 weeks. Use it on other sandwiches or in place of hummus as a vegetable dip.

---

10 oil-packed sun-dried tomatoes

1 cup sliced roasted red peppers

2 tablespoons water, plus more as needed

2 cloves garlic

¼ cup walnuts

¼ cup fresh mint

2 tablespoons fresh oregano

Pinch of cayenne pepper

Salt

4 (6") whole wheat pitas, cut in half

8 ounces cooked rotisserie chicken

1½ cups arugula

1 avocado, sliced

Soak the sun-dried tomatoes in a bowl of warm water for 30 minutes.

In a food processor, combine the tomatoes, ⅓ cup of the red peppers, the water, garlic, walnuts, mint, oregano, cayenne, and salt to taste. Process until smooth, scraping down the bowl as necessary. If the spread is too thick, add more water, 1 teaspoon at a time.

Place 1 tablespoon of the tomato spread in each pita half. Stuff each pita with an equal amount of the chicken, arugula, avocado, and remaining ⅔ cup red pepper.

NUTRITION PER SERVING: 382 calories, 43 g carbs, 9 g fiber, 26 g protein, 13 g total fat, 2 g saturated fat, 704 mg sodium

mediterranean pizza with smoked ham

Recipe by Matthew Kadey, MS, RD

makes 4 servings

total time: 15 minutes

Yes, you can enjoy pizza without it sabotaging your diet for the day—and, yes, it can even provide a health boost. Whole wheat pizza crust packs more fiber and B vitamins (which help a runner's body generate energy during workouts) than crust made with refined flour. Smoked ham is a leaner topping choice than bacon but still provides plenty of rich, meaty flavor.

---

1 thin (12") whole wheat pizza crust

¼ to ⅓ cup Kale-Almond Pesto (page 142) or jarred pesto

1 cup arugula or baby spinach

6 ounces uncured smoked ham, coarsely chopped

⅔ cup jarred sliced roasted red peppers

⅓ cup sliced olives (optional)

½ cup torn fresh basil

4 ounces goat cheese, crumbled

Ground black pepper

Preheat the oven to 400°F. Place the pizza crust on a baking sheet and bake for 6 minutes. Remove and turn the oven to broil.

Spread the pesto on the crust. Top with the arugula or spinach, ham, red peppers, olives (if using), basil, and goat cheese. Season to taste with black pepper. Broil for 1 minute, or until the toppings are hot.

NUTRITION PER SERVING: 427 calories, 37 g carbs, 7 g fiber, 29 g protein, 21 g total fat, 10 g saturated fat, 823 mg sodium

fig and prosciutto sandwich

Recipe by Matthew Kadey, MS, RD

makes 2 servings

total time: 20 minutes

Dried figs are surprisingly rich in minerals, including iron, calcium, manganese, and potassium. The latter, an electrolyte, works with sodium to maintain the body's fluid balance. Prosciutto provides a salty counterbalance to the sweet figs, making this electrolyte-rich pairing ideal before or after a sweaty run. Save any of the leftover homemade fig jam in the refrigerator to spread on sandwiches and toast. Or save time and use store-bought jam instead.

FIG JAM

- ½ **cup dried figs, coarsely chopped**
- ½ **cup apple cider**
- 1 **teaspoon honey**
- 1 **tablespoon lemon juice**
- ¼ **teaspoon ground cinnamon**

SANDWICH

- 2 **small whole wheat baguettes or other whole wheat roll, cut in half**
- 2 **slices prosciutto (1 ounce each)**
- 2 **slices Swiss cheese**
- ¼ **cup sliced roasted red peppers**
- ⅓ **cup baby spinach**

TO MAKE THE FIG JAM: In a saucepan, combine the figs and apple cider. Bring to a boil, reduce the heat to medium-low, and simmer, covered, for 10 minutes. Allow to cool slightly. Transfer to a blender or food processor along with the honey, lemon juice, and cinnamon. Blend for 1 minute, or until smooth.

TO MAKE THE SANDWICH: Spread 2 tablespoons fig jam on half of each baguette. (Reserve the leftover jam in the refrigerator.) Top each with 1 slice prosciutto, 1 slice cheese, half the red peppers, half the spinach, and then the other half of the baguettes.

NUTRITION PER SERVING: 363 calories, 45 g carbs, 4 g fiber, 21 g protein, 11 g total fat, 6 g saturated fat, 1,262 mg sodium

smoked salmon and veggie wrap

Recipe by Matthew Kadey, MS, RD

makes 4 servings

total time: 10 minutes

A plain bagel with cream cheese and lox can easily cost you more than 600 calories and 25 grams of fat, with nearly half of that fat coming from the unhealthy saturated kind—not exactly what you'd call runner-friendly fuel. This healthier take on that brunch staple swaps out the oversized bagel for a carb-rich whole grain wrap and uses low-fat cream cheese, saving you 200 calories and 10 grams of fat per serving.

½ cup low-fat cream cheese

2 tablespoons chopped dill

2 tablespoons chopped fresh chives

¼ teaspoon ground black pepper

4 whole grain wraps

8 ounces smoked salmon

2 tablespoons jarred capers

3 tablespoons sunflower seeds

1 cup sliced artichoke hearts

2 cups baby spinach

In a bowl, mix the cream cheese, dill, chives, and pepper. Spread on the wraps.

Top each wrap with an equal amount of the salmon, capers, sunflower seeds, artichoke hearts, and spinach. Roll up like a log and cut in 1½" slices.

NUTRITION PER SERVING: 397 calories, 30 g carbs, 7 g fiber, 43 g protein, 15 g total fat, 4.5 g saturated fat, 514 mg sodium

salmon salad sandwich with chili aioli

Recipe by Matthew Kadey, MS, RD

makes 2 servings

total time: 10 minutes

Tired of your usual tuna salad sandwich? Try swapping it out for one made of salmon. It contains more inflammation-calming omega-3s that can help reduce joint pain. Sweet-and-spicy sriracha (which is widely available in most supermarkets) provides a big boost of flavor for nearly zero calories. Rye bread contains up to 5 grams of fiber per slice—more than whole wheat. Just make sure the first ingredient on the loaf is whole rye flour or rye meal.

3 tablespoons mayonnaise

1 teaspoon sriracha or other hot chili sauce

5 ounces canned salmon

Juice of ½ lemon

2 tablespoons chopped fresh dill

1 clove garlic, minced

4 slices rye bread

⅔ to 1 cup arugula

½ tomato, sliced

In a small bowl, mix together the mayonnaise and sriracha. In another bowl, combine the salmon, lemon juice, dill, and garlic.

Divide the salmon mixture between 2 slices of rye bread. Top each with half the arugula and tomato slices.

Spread the mayo mixture on the other 2 slices of rye. Place those slices on top of the sandwiches.

NUTRITION PER SERVING: 425 calories, 35 g carbs, 4 g fiber, 23 g protein, 22 g total fat, 3 g saturated fat, 877 mg sodium

anchovy and olive pizza

Recipe by Matthew Kadey, MS, RD

makes 4 servings

total time: 10 minutes

They may be small in size, but anchovies pack robust, savory flavor—and a ton of nutrients—in a tiny package. The canned fillets are a good source of heart-healthy omega-3 fats, the B vitamin niacin, and selenium, which may play a role in joint health. They're also an environmentally friendly choice. If anchovies aren't your thing, swap them out for milder-tasting canned sardines.

- 2 cans (2 ounces each) oil-packed anchovies, or one 5-ounce can sardines, rinsed
- 4 (6") whole wheat pitas
- 2 teaspoons extra-virgin olive oil
- ½ cup jarred pizza sauce
- 16 pitted kalamata olives, rinsed and chopped
- 2 artichoke hearts, chopped (2 ounces)
- ⅛ teaspoon red-pepper flakes
- ½ cup shredded mozzarella cheese (2 ounces)
- Fresh basil leaves, torn

Preheat the broiler. Coarsely chop the anchovies or sardines.

Brush the pitas with the oil. Place on a baking sheet and broil on high 6" from the heat source for 2 minutes, or until golden brown on top.

Spread the pizza sauce over each pita. Top with the anchovies or sardines, olives, artichoke hearts, pepper flakes, and cheese. Broil for 1 minute, or until the cheese is melted. Garnish with the basil.

NUTRITION PER SERVING: 288 calories, 31 g carbs, 5 g fiber, 14 g protein, 13 g total fat, 3.5 g saturated fat, 1,393 mg sodium

bean and shrimp quesadilla

Recipe by Liz Applegate, PhD

makes 2 servings

total time: 15 minutes

Cooked shrimp and canned refried beans make for a quick carb- and protein-packed lunch or dinner. The combo also provides a triple shot of key runner-friendly minerals—calcium and magnesium for strong bones and iron to maintain endurance. Look for cooked shrimp in the frozen food aisle or at the fresh fish counter.

2 (8") whole wheat tortillas

1 cup canned low-sodium refried beans

6 ounces cooked small shrimp

¼ cup shredded Monterey Jack cheese

Couple sprigs of fresh cilantro, chopped

6 tablespoons tomato salsa

½ avocado, sliced

In a medium skillet, heat the tortillas, one at a time, over medium-high heat for 1 minute, turning over once.

Divide the beans in half and spread them on one half of each tortilla. Top each with half the shrimp, cheese, cilantro, salsa, and avocado.

Fold the tortillas in half. Put one in the skillet and heat for 2 minutes, or until slightly brown. Flip and heat for 1 or 2 minutes, or until the cheese is melted. Repeat with the remaining tortilla.

NUTRITION PER SERVING: 509 calories, 50 g carbs, 13 g fiber, 38 g protein, 19 g total fat, 5 g saturated fat, 973 mg sodium

white bean–artichoke wrap

Recipe by Matthew Kadey, MS, RD

makes 2 servings

total time: 10 minutes

Whole grain wraps are a smart choice for runners keeping an eye on calories. They have about 20 percent fewer calories than 2 slices of bread but still provide plenty of energizing carbohydrates. Make extra of this quick-and-easy bean spread to serve with pita chips and sliced vegetables.

1 can (15 ounces) no-salt-added white navy beans, drained and rinsed

3 tablespoons extra-virgin olive oil

2 cloves garlic

Juice of ½ lemon

1 tablespoon fresh thyme or 1 teaspoon dried

½ teaspoon paprika

½ teaspoon ground cumin

⅛ teaspoon salt

⅛ teaspoon ground black pepper

2 (7") whole grain tortillas

⅓ cup quartered artichoke hearts in water, drained

¼ cup fresh flat-leaf parsley

¼ cup sliced roasted red peppers

In a food processor, combine the beans, oil, garlic, lemon juice, thyme, paprika, cumin, salt, and black pepper. Process until smooth.

Spread the mixture evenly over the tortillas. Top each with an equal amount of the artichoke hearts, parsley, and red peppers. Roll up and slice each tortilla in half.

NUTRITION PER SERVING: 481 calories, 53 g carbs, 13 g fiber, 14 g protein, 25 g total fat, 4.5 g saturated fat, 741 mg sodium

caramelized onion and fig pizza

Recipe by Deena Kastor

makes 6 servings

total time: 45 minutes

"My two passions are running and food," says three-time Olympian Deena Kastor, who holds the American marathon record, "and they play off each other. If you fuel yourself with wholesome foods, your body will perform well." The key to good cooking, she says, is to start with good ingredients, and there are three she says she couldn't live without: balsamic vinegar, goat cheese, and arugula—all of which she incorporates into this easy, delicious, sweet-yet-savory pizza.

- 1 refrigerated ready-to-bake pizza dough
- 1 tablespoon extra-virgin olive oil
- 2 yellow onions, chopped
- ½ teaspoon salt
- 1 tablespoon packed brown sugar
- 1 tablespoon balsamic vinegar, plus more for drizzling
- 1 cup packed arugula leaves
- 6 dried figs, sliced
- 4 ounces goat cheese, crumbled

Preheat the oven to 450°F. Roll out the dough according to package instructions to fit a round or rectangular baking pan.

In a skillet over medium heat, combine the oil, onions, and salt. Cook, stirring occasionally, for 10 minutes, or until brown. Add the sugar and vinegar. Cook for 10 minutes, or until the onions are deep brown and very soft.

Spread the onion mixture over the dough, leaving an edge for the crust. Top with the arugula, figs, and goat cheese. Bake for 15 minutes, or until the crust is golden. Remove from the oven. Drizzle balsamic vinegar on top.

NUTRITION PER SERVING: 179 calories, 17 g carbs, 2 g fiber, 7 g protein, 10 g total fat, 5 g saturated fat, 305 mg sodium

almond butter and pear sandwich

Recipe by Matthew Kadey, MS, RD

makes 2 servings

total time: 10 minutes

Give your usual PB&J an upgrade with this more grown-up combo. Compared to peanut butter, almond butter contains more of the bone-building minerals calcium, magnesium, and phosphorus. While both spreads have a similar amount of total fat, the almond variety has more monounsaturated fat, which can help improve blood cholesterol levels. If you have time, try making your own using the recipe for Roasted Almond Butter on page 51.

- **3 tablespoons Roasted Almond Butter (page 51) or store-bought almond butter**
- **1 teaspoon honey**
- **¼ teaspoon ground cinnamon**
- **¼ teaspoon vanilla extract**
- **4 slices whole grain bread**
- **8 thin pear slices**
- **4 tablespoons chopped dried apricots**
- **4 tablespoons crumbled goat cheese**

In a small bowl, stir together the almond butter, honey, cinnamon, and vanilla extract. Spread the mixture on 2 slices of bread. Top the bread slices with an equal amount of the pear, dried apricot, and goat cheese. Top each with a second slice of bread.

NUTRITION PER SERVING: 451 calories, 48 g carbs, 7 g fiber, 16 g protein, 23 g total fat, 7 g saturated fat, 450 mg sodium

curry egg salad sandwich

Recipe by Matthew Kadey, MS, RD

makes 2 servings

total time: 10 minutes

Most deli-made egg salad is loaded with so much high-fat mayonnaise that it practically negates all the health-boosting benefits of eating nutrient-rich eggs, which are high in protein, vitamin D, and vitamin B$_{12}$. Swapping out the mayo for a touch of low-fat Greek yogurt gives egg salad the same velvety smooth texture and more protein with a fraction of the fat. Curry powder and raisins add an unexpected punch of flavor and antioxidants.

- ¼ cup low-fat plain Greek yogurt
- 2 tablespoons golden raisins
- 1 teaspoon Dijon mustard
- 2 scallions, sliced
- ½ teaspoon curry powder
- ⅛ teaspoon salt
- ⅛ teaspoon ground black pepper
- 4 egss, hard-cooked and chopped
- 2 whole grain bagels, cut in half
- 4 slices avocado
- ¼ cup fresh cilantro, coarsely chopped

In a bowl, stir together the yogurt, raisins, mustard, scallions, curry powder, salt, and pepper. Gently stir in the hard-cooked eggs.

Divide the egg mixture between 2 bagel halves. Top each with an equal amount of avocado and cilantro. Top with the remaining bagel halves.

NUTRITION PER SERVING: 421 calories, 51 g carbs, 9 g fiber, 22 g protein, 17 g total fat, 4 g saturated fat, 545 mg sodium

6

Sauces
and Pasta

Pasta Sauces

Pasta Dishes

quick-and-easy marinara

Recipe by Matthew Kadey, MS, RD

makes 4 servings

total time: 35 minutes

While all tomatoes are at their flavor peak in the summer, fresh plum tomatoes—with their meaty texture and low moisture content—can make good tomato sauce year-round. This recipe will also work with canned tomatoes if you don't have fresh on hand. Make a double batch, serve some over pasta for a prerun meal, and freeze the leftover sauce for dinner another night.

- **1 pound plum tomatoes, or 1 can (15 ounces) diced or crushed tomatoes**
- **4 cloves garlic, very coarsely chopped**
- **1 tablespoon balsamic vinegar**
- **1 teaspoon dried oregano**
- **½ teaspoon salt, plus more if needed**
- **3 tablespoons extra-virgin olive oil**

Slice the tops off the tomatoes (if using fresh) and discard. Cut the tomatoes into quarters. In a food processor, combine the tomatoes, garlic, vinegar, oregano, and salt. Process until smooth.

Transfer to a medium saucepan over medium heat. Stir in the oil. Raise the heat to high and bring the sauce to a boil. Reduce the heat to low and simmer for 30 minutes, or until slightly thickened. Taste and adjust for seasoning, if necessary.

NUTRITION PER SERVING: 123 calories, 7 g carbs, 2 g fiber, 1 g protein, 10 g total fat, 1.5 g saturated fat, 299 mg sodium

fire-roasted meat sauce

Recipe by Matthew Kadey, MS, RD

makes 6 servings

total time: 1 hour 15 minutes

Red-pepper flakes and canned fire-roasted tomatoes add big flavor to this rich, meaty sauce, perfect for dinner after a long run. While the recipe does take a little over an hour from start to finish, the sauce is gently simmering on the stove for most of that time, requiring little more than the occasional stir.

- **1 pound 85% lean ground beef**
- **1 onion, chopped**
- **1 red bell pepper, chopped**
- **3 cloves garlic, minced**
- **1 can (28 ounces) diced fire-roasted tomatoes**
- **1 can (5 ounces) tomato paste**
- **1 teaspoon dried oregano**
- **1 teaspoon dried basil**
- **½ teaspoon red-pepper flakes**
- **½ teaspoon salt**
- **½ teaspoon ground black pepper**
- **⅓ cup red wine**
- **1 tablespoon sugar**

Heat a large saucepan over medium-high heat. Add the ground beef and cook for 5 minutes, or until the pink disappears, breaking up the beef.

Add the onion, bell pepper, and garlic, and cook for 3 minutes, or until the onion and pepper are slightly softened.

Add the tomatoes, tomato paste, oregano, basil, pepper flakes, salt, black pepper, red wine, and sugar. Stir to combine. Once the sauce is bubbling, reduce the heat to low, and simmer, uncovered, for 1 hour.

NUTRITION PER SERVING: 249 calories, 17 g carbs, 3 g fiber, 17 g protein, 12 g total fat, 4.5 g saturated fat, 728 mg sodium

basil-mint pesto

Recipe by Pam Anderson

makes 5 servings

total time: 5 minutes

Pesto is traditionally made by grinding fresh basil leaves, pine nuts, garlic, olive oil, and Parmesan cheese into a paste. But the no-cook sauce can easily be adapted using whatever fresh herbs or nuts you prefer or have on hand. Runner's World contributing chef Pam Anderson likes to use mint in addition to basil in her pesto, to add refreshing flavor. Delicious on pasta, this pesto also goes well with roast lamb or pork.

¼ **cup pine nuts**

¼ **cup freshly grated Parmesan cheese**

¾ **cup fresh basil**

¼ **cup fresh mint**

3 **cloves garlic, very coarsely chopped**

¼ **cup extra-virgin olive oil**

Salt and ground black pepper

In a food processor, combine the pine nuts and cheese. Process until the nuts are broken into small pieces.

Add the basil, mint, and garlic. Process for 1 minute, or until the herbs are shredded and the garlic is minced. With the machine running, pour the oil through the feed tube and process, stopping to scrape down the sides of the bowl, for 30 seconds, or until the mixture is smooth. Season to taste with salt and pepper.

The pesto will last for about 1 week stored in a tightly sealed jar in the refrigerator. You can also freeze portions of the pesto in ice cube trays for later use (once frozen, put the cubes in a resealable plastic bag).

NUTRITION PER SERVING: 163 calories, 2 g carbs, 0 g fiber, 3 g protein, 17 g total fat, 2.5 g saturated fat, 178 mg sodium

kale-almond pesto

Recipe by Pam Anderson

makes 12 servings

total time: 15 minutes

Incredibly nutrient dense and low in calories, kale has earned its reputation as a superfood. One cup chopped provides well over 100 percent of your daily need for vitamins A and K, the latter of which is needed for bone health and blood clot formation. It also provides nearly 90 percent of your daily need for vitamin C, has 3 grams of fiber, and contains antioxidants that may protect against cancer and cardiovascular disease. Using it in pesto may be untraditional, but it makes a dark green, richly flavored—and nutrient-packed—sauce. While kale can sometimes be bitter, blanching the leaves takes care of this problem.

1 dozen large kale leaves

½ cup raw whole almonds

1 cup freshly grated Parmesan cheese

½ cup fresh basil leaves

3 cloves garlic, very coarsely chopped

½ cup cold water

Juice of ½ lemon

¼ teaspoon salt, plus more if needed

½ cup extra-virgin olive oil

Bring a large pot of water to a boil over high heat and set up a medium bowl of ice water. Add the kale to the boiling water and blanch for 4 minutes, or until bright green and tender. Remove and put into the bowl of ice water to stop the cooking process. Squeeze out the excess water, then pat the leaves dry. Cut out and discard the center ribs.

In a food processor, pulse the almonds to break them up. Then add the kale, cheese, basil, garlic, water, lemon juice, and salt. Pulse until roughly combined. With the machine running, pour in the oil. Continue to process until smooth, scraping down the sides of the bowl. Taste to adjust the seasoning.

The pesto will last for about 1 week stored in a tightly sealed jar in the refrigerator. Or freeze the pesto in ice cube trays, transfer to a resealable plastic bag, and use them as needed.

NUTRITION PER SERVING: 156 calories, 4 g carbs, 1 g fiber, 5 g protein, 14 g total fat, 3 g saturated fat, 161 mg sodium

cilantro-pumpkin pesto

Recipe by Matthew Kadey, MS, RD

makes 6 servings

total time: 5 minutes

Pungent-tasting cilantro might seem like an odd choice for pesto, but it creates a sauce with unmistakably fresh, herbal flavor. Cilantro is usually quite dirty when you buy it from the store, so be sure to rinse it under cold running water, or give it a few good swishes in a bowl of cold water, to remove all the grit. You can also eat cilantro stems, which makes prep very simple—just cut the stems at the base of the leaves and you're ready to go.

2 cups fresh cilantro

⅓ cup roasted pumpkin seeds

⅓ cup freshly grated Parmesan cheese

2 cloves garlic, very coarsely chopped

Juice of ½ lemon

¼ teaspoon salt

¼ cup extra-virgin olive oil

In a food processor, combine the cilantro, pumpkin seeds, cheese, garlic, lemon juice, and salt. Pulse until coarsely minced.

With the machine running, pour in the oil and process until well combined. Scrape down the sides of the bowl.

The pesto will last for about 1 week stored in a tightly sealed jar in the refrigerator. Or freeze the pesto in ice cube trays, transfer to a resealable bag, and use them as needed.

NUTRITION PER SERVING: 140 calories, 2 g carbs, 1 g fiber, 4 g protein, 14 g total fat, 2.5 g saturated fat, 277 mg sodium

tagliatelle with peas, chile, and mint

Recipe by Mark Bittman

makes 6 servings

total time: 25 minutes

Runner's World *contributing food writer Mark Bittman likes to make this spring pasta for a quick postrun lunch or supper. While some primavera recipes use a mishmash of vegetables tossed in a fatty cream sauce, Bittman's version highlights one fresh vegetable enhanced with just a touch of herbs and spices. One cup of peas contains nearly 100 percent of your daily need for vitamin C, 7 grams of fiber, and 45 percent of your daily need for bone-boosting vitamin K.*

Salt

2 cups shelled peas

1 pound tagliatelle (use linguine or fettuccine as a substitute)

3 tablespoons extra-virgin olive oil

1 tablespoon minced fresh hot chile (such as Thai) (wear plastic gloves while handling)

½ cup chopped fresh mint, plus more for garnish

½ cup freshly grated Pecorino Romano cheese, plus more for garnish

Bring a large pot of water to a boil over high heat and salt it. Add the shelled peas and cook for 3 to 5 minutes, or until tender. Remove the peas with a sieve. Add the tagliatelle to the boiling water.

Meanwhile, put 2 tablespoons of the oil in a medium saucepan over medium heat. When the oil is hot, add the chile and peas, and cook, stirring occasionally, for 2 minutes.

When the pasta is tender, drain it, reserving ¼ cup of the cooking water. Return the tagliatelle to the pot. Toss it with the remaining 1 tablespoon oil, the peas and chile, mint, and cheese. Add a bit of the cooking water, if you like, to wet the sauce. Serve garnished with more mint and cheese.

NUTRITION PER SERVING: 414 calories, 64 g carbs, 5 g fiber, 15 g protein, 11 g total fat, 3 g saturated fat, 223 mg sodium

bow-ties with tomato and arugula

Recipe by Mark Bittman

makes 4 servings

total time: 30 minutes

Juicy tomatoes, carb-rich grains, and salty olives and feta cheese make this bright and light Mediterranean dish satisfying after a long, hot run —or eat it the night before a run for a carbo-load. After you finish cooking, let it sit for a bit before serving, so that the bulgur and bow-ties soak up the flavors and the arugula wilts a little. It works equally well to serve this dish warm or at room temperature. For an earthier spin, try doubling the bulgur and reducing the quantity of pasta.

- **2 tablespoons extra-virgin olive oil**
- **1 small red onion, chopped**
- **1 tablespoon minced garlic**
- **1 cup mixed olives, pitted and coarsely chopped**
- **Juice of 1 lemon**
- **4 ripe tomatoes, cored and cut into thick wedges**
- **½ cup crumbled feta cheese**
- **Salt and ground black pepper**
- **¼ cup medium-grind (#2) bulgur**
- **8 ounces whole wheat bow-tie or other cut pasta**
- **3 cups torn arugula leaves**

Bring a large pot of water to a boil over high heat. Meanwhile, put the oil in a large, deep skillet over medium heat. When it's hot, add the onion and garlic and cook, stirring, for 5 minutes, or until they begin to soften. Stir in the olives, then add the lemon juice, tomatoes, and feta. Sprinkle with salt and pepper to taste, and cook until the tomatoes are just heated through. Turn off the heat.

When the water boils, salt it and add the bulgur. Let the water return to a boil, then add the pasta. Cook the bow-ties until they are tender (start tasting after 5 minutes). Reserve some of the cooking water, then drain in a strainer—not a colander—to trap the grains with the pasta.

Toss the pasta and bulgur with the tomato mixture, adding some of the cooking water, if necessary to wet the sauce. Stir in the arugula and taste and adjust the seasoning. Let the dish sit for up to 15 minutes. Stir again and serve.

NUTRITION PER SERVING: 456 calories, 61 g carbs, 9 g fiber, 14 g protein, 20 g total fat, 5 g saturated fat, 929 mg sodium

portobello and asparagus pasta

Recipe by Philippe Forcioli

makes 8 servings

total time: 25 minutes

Philippe Forcioli, chef and owner of GreenFire Market Organic and Natural Restaurant in Rockford, Illinois, and a runner, craves this carb-packed dish the night before a long run whenever he's in marathon training—which is often, considering he's run more than 25 of them. Mushrooms and asparagus provide B vitamins, and pesto contains heart-healthy, unsaturated fat. The pesto will keep in the refrigerator for a week.

PESTO

- ⅔ **cup pine nuts**
- 20 **large fresh basil leaves**
- ⅔ **cup fresh parsley**
- ½ **cup extra-virgin olive oil**
- ¼ **cup freshly grated Parmesan cheese**
- 4 **cloves garlic, very coarsely chopped**
- ½ **teaspoon salt**
- ¼ **teaspoon ground black pepper**

PASTA

- **Salt**
- 1½ **pounds shell or bow-tie pasta or tortellini**
- 32 **asparagus spears, chopped into bite-size pieces**
- 1 **tablespoon extra-virgin olive oil**
- 2 **large portobello mushroom caps, sliced (remove gills with a spoon)**
- 4 **teaspoons chopped fresh parsley**

Put a large pot of water over high heat to boil.

TO MAKE THE PESTO: In a food processor, combine the pine nuts, basil, ⅔ cup parsley, oil, cheese, garlic, salt, and pepper. Process until medium smooth.

TO MAKE THE PASTA: Once the water is boiling, salt it and add the pasta. Cook for 5 minutes, then add the asparagus.

Meanwhile, in a medium skillet, heat the oil over medium heat. Add the mushrooms and cook for 7 minutes, or until tender.

When the pasta is cooked al dente, strain it and the asparagus, reserving ½ cup of the cooking water. Return the pasta and asparagus to the pot along with ¼ cup of the reserved cooking water. Mix in the pesto. Stir in the remaining ¼ cup cooking water. Top the pasta with the mushrooms and sprinkle with the chopped parsley.

NUTRITION PER SERVING: 559 calories, 69 g carbs, 5 g fiber, 16 g protein, 26 g total fat, 3.5 g saturated fat, 244 mg sodium

pasta bean toss

makes 8 servings

total time: 35 minutes

Recipe by Joan Salge Blake, MS, RD, LDN

Whole grain pasta, beans, and plenty of fresh vegetables make this recipe a carb- and antioxidant-packed meal that will restock your energy stores after a run. It makes 8 hearty portions, so save any leftovers for lunch the next day. Cutting the vegetables the night before will help speed up the cooking process.

Salt

1 pound whole grain penne

1 tablespoon canola oil

1 red onion, thinly sliced

2 cloves garlic, minced

3 carrots, cut into matchsticks or thin coins

2 cups raw broccoli florets

12 fresh plum tomatoes, diced

3 tablespoons Worcestershire sauce

4 tablespoons chopped fresh basil or 2 tablespoons dried

1 can (15 ounces) red kidney beans, drained and rinsed

1 can (15 ounces) white kidney beans, drained and rinsed

½ cup freshly grated Parmesan cheese, plus more to serve

Bring a large pot of water to a boil over high heat. When it boils, salt the water and add the pasta. Cook according to package directions.

While the pasta cooks, heat the oil in a large skillet over medium-high heat. Add the onion and cook for 7 minutes, or until tender. Add the garlic and cook for 1 minute longer.

Add the carrots, broccoli, tomatoes, Worcestershire sauce, and basil. Cook for 4 minutes. Add the red and white beans and cook for 2 minutes, or until the vegetables are tender.

Drain the pasta and add it to the pan along with the cheese. Toss together and serve with additional Parmesan, if desired.

NUTRITION PER SERVING: 342 calories, 61 g carbs, 11 g fiber, 14 g protein, 5 g total fat, 1 g saturated fat, 303 mg sodium

penne with sardines, prosciutto, and cherry tomatoes

Recipe by Matthew Kadey, MS, RD

makes 6 servings

total time: 25 minutes

Salty prosciutto, juicy tomatoes, and crunchy walnuts are the perfect (if slightly unexpected) complement to meaty-tasting sardines. And if you've never eaten these little fish, it's time to give them a chance. Sardines provide a healthy dose of vitamin B_{12}, omega-3s, and vitamin D, which may play a key role in keeping your immune system running strong. They're also an environmentally friendly choice. You can buy sardines with or without the bones (the former does provide additional calcium), so choose whichever you prefer.

Salt

1 pound whole wheat penne

3 tins (4 ounces each) oil-packed sardines, drained

2 ounces prosciutto, diced

1 pint cherry tomatoes, halved

½ cup toasted walnuts

1 tablespoon fresh thyme, chopped

¼ cup extra-virgin olive oil

Juice of ½ lemon

3 cloves garlic, minced

¼ teaspoon ground black pepper

¼ teaspoon red-pepper flakes

Freshly grated Parmesan cheese

Bring a large pot of water to a boil over high heat. When it boils, salt the water and add the pasta. Cook according to package directions and drain when done.

Meanwhile, coarsely chop the sardines and put them in a large bowl. Add the cooked pasta, prosciutto, tomatoes, walnuts, and thyme.

In a small bowl, whisk together the olive oil, lemon juice, garlic, black pepper, and pepper flakes. Toss with the pasta mixture and garnish with the cheese.

NUTRITION PER SERVING: 547 calories, 61 g carbs, 8 g fiber, 25 g protein, 23 g total fat, 3 g saturated fat, 567 mg sodium

shrimp, artichoke, and pesto pasta

Recipe by Matthew Kadey, MS, RD

makes 4 servings

total time: 20 minutes

This pasta is a cinch to throw together with long-lasting kitchen staples, such as sun-dried tomatoes, jarred pesto, and frozen shrimp. A half cup of frozen artichoke hearts provides 6 grams of fiber and—unlike the jarred, marinated version—has a fresh, mildly sweet flavor with no added calories. While this dish is perfect for postrun recovery, it also makes an ideal carb-packed meal the night before a long run.

Salt

12 ounces whole grain spirals or shells

1 tablespoon extra-virgin olive oil

12 ounces frozen artichoke hearts

1 pound frozen peeled and deveined shrimp, thawed

¾ cup Cilantro-Pumpkin Pesto (page 143) or store-bought pesto

1 cup (2 ounces) sliced sun-dried tomatoes

Bring a large pot of water to a boil over high heat. When it boils, salt the water and add the pasta. Cook according to package directions and drain when done.

Meanwhile, heat the oil in a large skillet over medium heat. Add the artichoke hearts. Cook for 3 to 4 minutes, or until just about heated through.

Add the shrimp and cook for 2 minutes, or until the shrimp are just pink and cooked through. Add the cooked pasta, pesto, and sun-dried tomatoes. Toss to coat the pasta and vegetables with the pesto.

NUTRITION PER SERVING: 758 calories, 80 g carbs, 17 g fiber, 46 g protein, 30 g total fat, 6.5 g saturated fat, 960 mg sodium

soba noodles with chicken and peanut sauce

Recipe by Patricia Wells

makes 4 servings

total time: 20 minutes

This is a favorite weeknight dinner of cookbook author and runner Patricia Wells. The soba noodles are bathed in a rich sauce of soy, sesame, peanut butter, and vinegar with a hint of garlic and ginger. "Sliced scallions add the essential element of crunch," she says, "and the smoothness of the chicken is punctuated by a garnish of toasted sesame seeds, peanuts, and cilantro." Serve the dish at room temperature. With plenty of carbs, it's an ideal choice the night before a long run or for postrun recovery.

- 3 tablespoons reduced-sodium soy sauce or tamari
- 2 tablespoons sesame oil
- 1 tablespoon natural smooth peanut butter
- ¼ cup rice vinegar
- 2 tablespoons water
- 1 tablespoon grated fresh ginger
- 2 cloves garlic, minced
- 10 ounces soba noodles
- 2 cups shredded cooked chicken, warmed or at room temperature
- 5 scallions, green and white parts, thinly sliced
- ¼ cup toasted sesame seeds
- ¼ cup chopped unsalted peanuts
- ¼ cup fresh cilantro leaves

In a large, shallow bowl, whisk the soy sauce or tamari, sesame oil, peanut butter, vinegar, water, ginger, and garlic.

In a large pot, boil 3 quarts of water. Add the soba noodles and stir. Cook for 5 minutes, or until tender. Drain in a colander and run hot water over the noodles until the water runs clear. (If the noodles aren't rinsed, they'll become starchy and sticky.) Drain thoroughly again.

Add the noodles to the sauce and toss to coat evenly. Add the chicken and scallions and toss again. Garnish with the sesame seeds, peanuts, and cilantro.

NUTRITION PER SERVING: 571 calories, 60 g carbs, 3 g fiber, 39 g protein, 21 g total fat, 3 g saturated fat, 1,081 mg sodium

penne with turkey-feta meatballs

Recipe by Pam Anderson

makes 6 servings

total time: 1 hour 15 minutes

Runner's World *contributing chef Pam Anderson likes to make this crowd-pleasing, healthy take on an Italian classic for her family. High in protein and carbs, it's ideal fuel after a long run. Adding a bit of feta cheese to lean ground turkey creates a flavorful meatball that also stays moist when cooked.*

---

8 cloves garlic (3 whole, 5 minced)

1½ pounds ground turkey

¾ cup crumbled feta cheese, plus more for garnish

½ cup crumbled saltines

½ teaspoon dried oregano

1 egg

1 tablespoon tomato paste

¼ cup extra-virgin olive oil

4 slices (2 ounces) prosciutto, chopped

1 cup red wine

2 cans (28 ounces) no-salt-added crushed tomatoes

7 cups water

½ teaspoon salt, plus more if needed

1 pound penne

Heat a large skillet over medium-high heat. Add the whole garlic cloves and toast for 5 minutes. Remove from the skillet, then smash and mince them.

Break up the turkey in a large bowl. Add the feta, saltines, and oregano. Gently mix together.

In a small bowl, mix together the egg, tomato paste, and toasted garlic. Add to the meat mixture and thoroughly combine. Form into 24 meatballs.

Heat the oil in a large pot over medium heat. Add the meatballs (working in batches) and brown on two sides. Transfer to a plate.

Add the minced garlic and prosciutto to the pot. Cook, stirring frequently, for 1 minute, or until the garlic is golden. Add the wine and reduce by half. Add the tomatoes and 1 cup of water to thin the sauce. Bring to a simmer. Add the meatballs to the sauce and cook, loosely covered, for 15 minutes.

Add the remaining 6 cups water to the same pot, along with the salt. Bring to a simmer. Add the penne, cover loosely, and cook, stirring frequently, for 15 minutes, or until the pasta is tender. Uncover and simmer until the sauce thickens. Adjust the seasoning to taste. Garnish each portion with feta and serve.

NUTRITION PER SERVING: 731 calories, 81 g carbs, 7 g fiber, 43 g protein, 23 g total fat, 7 g saturated fat, 821 mg sodium

rigatoni with chicken sausage

Recipe by Melissa Lasher

makes 6 servings
total time: 20 minutes

Chicken sausage is typically leaner than pork versions but still provides plenty of rich, meaty flavor and protein for muscle recovery. Look for already cooked sausage at the supermarket to save on prep time. Using frozen vegetables also helps get this meal on the table in a hurry, while a generous amount of basil adds fresh summertime flavor.

Salt

12 ounces rigatoni

3 tablespoons extra-virgin olive oil

4 cups (12 ounces) frozen broccoli florets

2 cups (8 ounces) frozen sliced red bell peppers

4 cooked chicken sausages (3 ounces each), sliced into ¼" thick rounds

½ cup chopped fresh basil

½ cup (2½ ounces) crumbled feta cheese

Ground black pepper

Bring a large pot of water to a boil over high heat. When boiling, salt the water and add the rigatoni. Cook according to package directions, then drain, reserving 1 cup of the cooking water.

Meanwhile, heat 1½ tablespoons of the oil in a large skillet over medium-high heat. Add the broccoli and bell peppers. Cover and cook, stirring occasionally, for 6 to 7 minutes, or until the vegetables are heated through. Remove them from the skillet.

Add the remaining 1½ tablespoons oil to the skillet. Add the sausages and cook for 5 minutes, or until lightly browned. (Work in batches, if necessary.)

Add the cooked rigatoni, reserved cooking water, and vegetables to the skillet. Top with the basil, feta, and black pepper to taste.

NUTRITION PER SERVING: 415 calories, 48 g carbs, 4 g fiber, 21 g protein, 15 g total fat, 4.5 g saturated fat, 537 mg sodium

quick 'n' creamy chicken lasagna

Recipe by Pam Anderson

makes 12 servings

total time: 1 hour 20 minutes

"Short of buying it premade, this lasagna is about the simplest there is," says Runner's World *contributing chef Pam Anderson. It's also one of the tastiest, thanks to the combination of cream cheese and mozzarella. If you want to make a lower-fat version, you can also use reduced-fat cream cheese or swap half the cream cheese for part-skim ricotta. For a vegetarian version, try the spinach-mushroom filling.*

---

15 oven-ready, rippled-style lasagna noodles (you'll need two 8-ounce boxes)

4 cups filling (see recipes below)

1½ teaspoons dried basil

12 ounces cream cheese, softened

½ cup chicken or vegetable broth

4 cups marinara sauce

4 cups shredded mozzarella cheese

¾ cup freshly grated Parmesan cheese

Chicken Filling
Shred 4 cups cooked chicken in a medium bowl.

Spinach-Mushroom Filling
Heat 2 tablespoons extra-virgin olive oil in a large skillet over medium-high heat. Add 1 pound sliced mushrooms. Cook until tender and well browned, 5 to 7 minutes. Add 2 (10-ounce) packages thawed and squeezed-dry chopped frozen spinach. Continue to cook until heated through. Transfer to a medium bowl.

Adjust the oven rack to the lower-middle position and preheat the oven to 400°F.

Put 2 quarts of piping hot tap water in a 13" x 9" baking dish. Add the noodles and soak for 10 minutes, or until soft. Drain and set the noodles aside.

Meanwhile, prepare your choice of filling. Combine the filling with the basil, 8 ounces of the cream cheese, and ¼ cup of the broth.

In a small bowl, mix the remaining 4 ounces cream cheese with the remaining ¼ cup broth.

To assemble the lasagna, smear ¼ cup marinara sauce on the bottom of the baking dish, then assemble 4 layers in the following order: 3 lasagna noodles, a scant cup of marinara sauce, 1 cup of the chicken filling or a scant cup of the spinach-mushroom filling, ¾ cup mozzarella cheese, and 2 tablespoons Parmesan cheese.

Once assembled, top the lasagna with the remaining 3 noodles, the cream cheese-broth mixture, ¾ cup mozzarella, and ¼ cup Parmesan.

Cover the lasagna with foil coated with cooking spray. Bake for 40 to 45 minutes, or until bubbly throughout. Leaving the lasagna on the same rack, turn the oven to broil. Remove the foil and broil for 4 to 5 minutes, or until the lasagna is spotty brown. Remove from the oven. Let sit for 10 minutes, then cut into squares and serve.

NUTRITION PER SERVING (CHICKEN VERSION): 470 calories, 27 g carbs, 3 g fiber, 31 g protein, 26 g total fat, 12.5 g saturated fat, 847 mg sodium

NUTRITION PER SERVING (SPINACH-MUSHROOM VERSION): 439 calories, 30 g carbs, 4 g fiber, 19 g protein, 26 g total fat, 12 g saturated fat, 991 mg sodium

7

Meat and Poultry Mains

grilled beef fajitas

Recipe by Carrie Tollefson

makes 6 servings

total time: 1 hour 25 minutes (including marinating time)

Beef is one of the richest sources of iron, which helps promote healthy red blood cells that transport oxygen to muscles. Without enough of this key mineral, runners can develop anemia, which causes fatigue and hinders performance. Years ago, when 2004 Olympian Carrie Tollefson had a bout with anemia, she decided to start eating beef three times a week, which helped her build her iron reserves back up. Grass-fed beef is a particularly healthy choice, since it contains less total fat than conventionally raised beef and has more omega-3 fatty acids. "This beef fajita recipe is a favorite of mine," says Tollefson. "It's an easy dinner and it makes great leftovers for lunch."

½ **cup chopped fresh cilantro**

Juice of 2 limes

½ **teaspoon ground cumin**

½ **teaspoon granulated garlic, or ¼ teaspoon garlic powder**

½ **teaspoon paprika**

2 **cloves garlic, minced**

2 **pounds flank steak**

1 **tablespoon extra-virgin olive oil**

2 **green or red bell peppers, cut into thin strips**

1 **large onion, thinly sliced**

18 **small (6") corn tortillas**

2 **tomatoes, diced**

1 **avocado, diced**

Combine the cilantro, lime juice, cumin, granulated garlic or garlic powder, paprika, and minced garlic in a large resealable plastic bag. Seal the bag and shake it to mix the ingredients. Open the bag and add the flank steak. Seal the bag again and turn to coat the meat with the mixture. Put the bag in the refrigerator and let the meat marinate for 40 minutes, being sure to turn it over at least once.

Meanwhile, heat the oil in a large skillet over medium-high heat. Add the bell peppers and cook, stirring frequently, for 5 to 8 minutes, or until softened and beginning to brown. Transfer the peppers to a serving bowl.

Add the onion to the skillet and cook, stirring frequently, for 10 minutes, or until softened and beginning to brown. Transfer the onion to a separate serving bowl.

When the meat is done marinating, coat a grill rack with cooking spray and preheat the grill. Cook the meat over medium-high heat for 7 minutes per side, or until medium-rare. Remove the meat from the grill and let it rest for 5 minutes.

Meanwhile, warm the tortillas for about 5 minutes in a warm oven or 30 seconds in a microwave on high power. Put the tomatoes in a small serving bowl. Place the avocado in another small serving bowl.

Thinly slice the meat and serve it with the fajita fixings and the tortillas.

NUTRITION PER SERVING: 608 calories, 52 g carbs, 6 g fiber, 46 g protein, 23 g total fat, 7 g saturated fat, 194 mg sodium

marinated beef and veggie kebabs

Recipe by Liz Applegate, PhD

makes 4 servings

total time: 1 hour 25 minutes (including marinating time)

Serve these kebabs at your next postrace cookout. Antioxidant-packed vegetables and protein-rich beef are the ideal combination to help speed recovery. While both top sirloin and sirloin are lean cuts of beef, the former contains fewer calories and less fat than the latter. The kebabs can be assembled a few hours before cooking. If you use wooden skewers, be sure to soak them in water for an hour or two before using.

- **1 teaspoon peeled and grated fresh ginger**
- **3 tablespoons reduced-sodium soy sauce**
- **½ cup dry white wine**
- **1 tablespoon honey**
- **1 tablespoon extra-virgin olive oil**
- **1 pound top sirloin steak or sirloin steak, trimmed of fat, cut into 1½" cubes**
- **1 red bell pepper, cut into 12 chunks**
- **1 yellow bell pepper, cut into 12 chunks**
- **1 small eggplant, cut into 12 cubes**
- **1 red onion, cut into 12 chunks**
- **Salt and ground black pepper**

Combine the ginger, soy sauce, wine, honey, and oil in a large resealable plastic bag. Seal the bag and shake it to mix the ingredients. Open the bag and add the beef, red and yellow bell peppers, eggplant, and onion. Seal it again and toss to coat with the marinade. Place the bag in the refrigerator and let it marinate for 1 hour, turning the bag over occasionally.

Coat a grill rack with cooking spray and preheat the grill to medium-high. Assemble the kebabs on four 12" metal skewers or eight 6" wooden skewers (soak them in water for an hour or two before using), threading a few pieces of vegetables in between pieces of beef. Don't overcrowd the skewers. Season to taste with salt and pepper.

Grill the kebabs over medium-high heat, turning once or twice, for 8 minutes for medium-rare or 11 minutes for well-done, or until desired doneness.

NUTRITION PER SERVING: 377 calories, 19 g carbs, 5 g fiber, 25 g protein, 20 g total fat, 7 g saturated fat, 640 mg sodium

meat loaf

Recipe by Liz Applegate, PhD

makes 6 servings

total time: 1 hour 15 minutes

Traditional meat loaf may be one of the ultimate comfort foods, but it's also usually high in unhealthy saturated fat. Using extra-lean ground beef slashes the fat content, while adding oat bran and plenty of vegetables ups the fiber and keeps calories in check (while also keeping the loaf moist). If you don't have oat bran on hand, try using wheat germ, ground flaxseed, or whole wheat bread crumbs.

---

1 onion, cut in half

1 rib celery, cut in half

1 carrot, cut in half

2 cloves garlic

¼ cup fresh parsley

¼ teaspoon cayenne pepper

¼ to ⅓ cup low-fat milk

1 egg, lightly beaten

½ cup oat bran

1 pound 95% lean ground beef

4 tablespoons tomato paste

¼ cup ketchup (optional)

Preheat the oven to 375°F. Coat a 13" x 9" pan or large glass baking dish with cooking spray.

In a food processor, combine the onion, celery, carrot, garlic, parsley, and cayenne. Process until the vegetables are finely chopped. Transfer to a large bowl.

In a small bowl, combine the milk, egg, and oat bran. Let stand for a few minutes to allow the oat bran to absorb the wet ingredients.

Add the beef, oat bran mixture, and tomato paste to the bowl with the chopped vegetables. Gently but thoroughly combine the mixture with your hands.

Form the meat mixture into a loaf shape. Place the loaf in the baking dish. Spread the top of the loaf with ketchup, if using. Bake for 1 hour, or until a thermometer inserted into the center of the loaf reads 165°F.

NUTRITION PER SERVING: 165 calories, 11 g carbs, 3 g fiber, 20 g protein, 65 g total fat, 2 g saturated fat, 171 mg sodium

barbecue beef sloppy joes

Recipe by the Rodale Test Kitchen

makes 6 servings

total time: 30 minutes

You may think of sloppy Joes as kids' food, but there's no reason why this old-school favorite can't be on a runner's menu. In fact, when made with extra-lean ground beef, it's a rich source of protein for muscle recovery, zinc to support a strong immune system, and iron to sustain endurance. Serve it on a whole grain bun and you'll get plenty of fiber-rich complex carbs, too. Chipotle chile powder packs a strong kick, so start by adding less and adjust to suit your tastes. Pair the sandwich with Fresh Market Slaw (page 75) for a tasty recovery meal.

- 1½ pounds 95% lean ground beef
- ½ cup tomato puree
- ½ cup apple juice
- 2 tablespoons maple syrup
- 1 to 2 teaspoons chipotle chile powder
- ½ teaspoon salt
- ½ teaspoon ground black pepper
- 1 small yellow onion, chopped
- 6 whole wheat hamburger buns

Brown the beef in a large skillet over medium heat. Add the tomato puree, apple juice, maple syrup, chile powder (to taste), salt, and black pepper. Stir to combine with the meat. Add the onion. Cover and simmer on low for 20 minutes. Serve on the hamburger buns.

NUTRITION PER SERVING: 306 calories, 31 g carbs, 4 g fiber, 29 g protein, 8 g total fat, 3 g saturated fat, 559 mg sodium

thai beef and snow pea stir-fry

Recipe by Liz Applegate, PhD

makes 4 servings

total time: 30 minutes

This tasty carbohydrate-and-protein combo makes a perfect postworkout dinner to refuel depleted muscles. You can have this quick-and-easy stir-fry ready in less time than it takes to cook the noodles.

Salt

1 package (9 ounces) soba noodles or whole wheat spaghetti

1 tablespoon canola oil

¾ pound sirloin beef, thinly sliced into 2" pieces

½ pound snow peas, trimmed

½ cup bottled Thai peanut sauce, or use the Peanut Dressing recipe on page 70

1 can (8 ounces) sliced water chestnuts, drained

Bring a large pot of water to a boil over high heat. When it boils, salt the water and add the noodles. Cook according to the package directions.

Meanwhile, in a large skillet, heat the oil over medium-high heat. Add the beef and cook, stirring frequently, for 3 minutes, or until lightly browned.

Add the snow peas and cook, stirring frequently, for 3 minutes. Add the peanut sauce or dressing, water chestnuts, and cooked noodles. Toss to coat everything with the sauce.

NUTRITION PER SERVING: 538 calories, 67 g carbs, 8 g fiber, 35 g protein, 15 g total fat, 6 g saturated fat, 257 mg sodium

stove-top pork and brown rice

Recipe by Matthew Kadey, MS, RD

makes 4 servings

total time: 55 minutes

Pork tenderloin is an exceptionally lean cut of meat. In fact, it has a 6-to-1 ratio of protein to fat calories, along with a high amount of selenium, an antioxidant that may ease exercise-induced oxidative stress in the body. Cooking the meat and rice together in a flavorful red wine–tomato sauce helps to keep the pork moist and tender.

- **1 tablespoon canola oil**
- **1 onion, diced**
- **1 pound pork tenderloin, cut into 2" cubes**
- **2 cloves garlic, minced**
- **1 cup dry red wine**
- **1 can (28 ounces) crushed tomatoes**
- **1 cup water**
- **1 cup brown rice**
- **1 red bell pepper, diced**
- **2 teaspoons Dijon mustard**
- **1 teaspoon dried oregano**
- **¼ teaspoon cayenne pepper**
- **¼ teaspoon salt**
- **¼ teaspoon ground black pepper**

In a large pot or Dutch oven, heat the oil over medium heat. Add the onion, pork, and garlic. Cook for 5 minutes, turning the pork to brown on all sides. Add the wine and simmer for 5 minutes.

Add the tomatoes, water, rice, bell pepper, mustard, oregano, cayenne, salt, and black pepper. Stir to combine. Bring to a boil over medium-high heat, then reduce the heat to low, cover, and simmer for 30 minutes, or until the rice is tender.

NUTRITION PER SERVING: 475 calories, 57 g carbs, 7 g fiber, 31 g protein, 9 g total fat, 2 g saturated fat, 429 mg sodium

pork tenderloin with winter vegetables

Recipe by Liz Applegate, PhD

makes 4 servings

total time: 55 minutes

While larger cuts of meat, like beef roast, can take hours to cook, pork tenderloin is ready in a fraction of that time. When paired with winter vegetables like sweet potatoes and carrots, it makes for an easy and satisfying dish after a cold-weather run. Feel free to use whatever hearty winter vegetables you like.

2 tablespoons Dijon mustard

2 cloves garlic, minced

¼ teaspoon ground black pepper

1 tablespoon extra-virgin olive oil

1 pound pork tenderloin

8 ounces Brussels sprouts, halved

1 sweet potato, cut into 1" chunks

1 small fennel bulb, cut into 2" chunks

2 carrots, cut into 1" chunks

1 cup chicken stock

Preheat the oven to 400°F. In a small bowl, mix together the mustard, garlic, and pepper.

In a medium skillet, heat the oil over medium-high heat. Add the pork and brown on all sides.

Set the pork in a 13" x 9" baking dish. Spread the mustard mixture over the top of the pork. Surround the meat with the Brussels sprouts, sweet potato, fennel, and carrots. Pour the stock over the vegetables and turn to coat.

Cook for 35 to 45 minutes, or until a thermometer inserted into the center of the meat reads 145°F.

NUTRITION PER SERVING: 239 calories, 18 g carbs, 5 g fiber, 27 g protein, 7 total fat, 1 g saturated fat, 565 mg sodium

mediterranean pork-asparagus stir-fry

Recipe by Matthew Kadey, MS, RD

makes 4 servings

total time: 55 minutes

Stir-fries may traditionally be an Asian dish, but there's no reason why you can't use the same fast, high-heat cooking technique to create meals with a different ethnic flare, like this Mediterranean-inspired dish. Pearled barley is a chewy, flavorful alternative to rice. It cooks faster than whole grain barley, but still provides loads of carbs, fiber, and vitamins.

1 cup pearled barley

2½ cups water

1 tablespoon canola oil

1 pound pork tenderloin, cut into thin slices

1 bunch asparagus, trimmed and cut into 1" pieces

⅓ cup pitted, chopped kalamata olives

⅓ cup chopped sun-dried tomatoes

2 tablespoons jarred capers

2 cloves garlic, sliced

¼ teaspoon salt

¼ teaspoon ground black pepper

¼ teaspoon red-pepper flakes

1 cup fresh flat-leaf parsley

2 tablespoons balsamic vinegar

In a medium pot, bring the barley and water to a boil over high heat. Reduce the heat to low and simmer, covered, for 40 minutes, or until tender.

Meanwhile, heat a wok or large skillet over medium-high heat. Add the oil and pork. Cook, stirring frequently, for 4 minutes, or until the meat is no longer pink. Remove from the wok and set on a plate.

Add the asparagus to the wok and cook, stirring frequently, for 3 minutes, or until tender. Add the olives, tomatoes, capers, garlic, salt, black pepper, and pepper flakes. Cook for 1 minute. Add the pork, parsley, and vinegar. Heat through for 30 seconds, tossing to combine. Serve over the barley.

NUTRITION PER SERVING: 450 calories, 50 g carbs, 11 g fiber, 32 g protein, 14 g total fat, 2 g saturated fat, 879 mg sodium

super-easy barbecue pulled pork

Recipe from The Rodale Test Kitchen

makes 6 servings

total time: 2 hours

Barbecued spareribs—a favorite at summer cookouts—can contain as much as 26 grams of fat per serving. Try this hearty, high-protein dish instead. It is just as satisfying and will fill you up with a fraction of the fat. While the dish takes 2 hours from start to finish, most of that time the pork cooks unattended. Serve it with a side of Creamy Coleslaw (page 74), corn on the cob, and a slice of fresh watermelon.

1 tablespoon extra-virgin olive oil

1½ pounds boneless pork loin, trimmed of all visible fat

1 onion, chopped (about ½ cup)

⅔ cup ketchup

1 tablespoon cider vinegar

1 tablespoon molasses

2 teaspoons packed brown sugar

2 teaspoons mustard powder

1½ teaspoons garlic powder

1 teaspoon Worcestershire sauce

¼ teaspoon ground black pepper

1½ cups chicken or vegetable broth

Heat the oil in a medium saucepan over medium-high heat. Add the pork and brown, turning occasionally, for 5 minutes.

Add the onion, ketchup, vinegar, molasses, sugar, mustard powder, garlic powder, Worcestershire sauce, pepper, and broth. Stir the mixture well to combine and bring to a boil over medium-high heat. Reduce the heat to low, cover, and simmer, stirring occasionally, for 1½ hours, or until the pork is very tender.

Uncover the saucepan, remove the pork to a cutting board, and loosely cover with foil. Continue to simmer the remaining sauce 10 minutes longer, or until the sauce has thickened slightly. Remove from the heat. Pull the pork into shreds with two forks and serve with the sauce.

NUTRITION PER SERVING: 218 calories, 13 g carbs, 1 g fiber, 25 g protein, 7 g total fat, 2 g saturated fat, 599 mg sodium

chicken not pie

Recipe by Mark Bittman

makes 4 servings

total time: 50 minutes

Traditional chicken potpie can take a long while to prepare, thanks to the labor involved in making the crust—which tastes delicious but adds refined carbs and saturated fat. Runner's World *contributing food writer Mark Bittman forgoes the high-fat crust and serves this meal atop brown rice, whole grain bread, or whole wheat fettuccine.*

- ¼ cup extra-virgin olive oil
- 2 leeks (including some of the green part), washed well, dried, and chopped
- ⅛ teaspoon salt, plus more if needed
- ⅛ teaspoon ground black pepper, plus more if needed
- 1 cup dry white wine or water
- 1 cup vegetable broth or more water
- ½ teaspoon chopped fresh thyme or tarragon leaves, or a good pinch of dried thyme or tarragon
- 2 boneless chicken breasts (6 ounces each), or 4 whole chicken tenderloins
- 2 or 3 large all-purpose potatoes, cut into 1" cubes
- 2 carrots or parsnips, cut into coins
- ½ pound sugar snap peas or snow peas, trimmed, or 1 cup peas (frozen are fine)
- ½ pound asparagus, cut into 1" pieces
- 2 tablespoons lemon juice
- Chopped fresh parsley

Pour half of the oil into a large skillet over medium heat. When the oil is hot, add the leeks, salt, and pepper and cook, stirring occasionally, for 5 minutes, or until softened. Add the wine or water, broth, and herbs. Bring to a boil and let bubble for 1 or 2 minutes.

Add the chicken, reduce the heat to medium-low, cover, and simmer for 5 or 6 minutes, or until the meat is barely cooked through. Remove the chicken from the skillet.

Add the potatoes and bring to a boil. Reduce the heat so the liquid bubbles enthusiastically. Cook for 5 minutes, or until the potatoes are almost tender. Stir in the carrots or parsnips and cook for another couple of minutes. By now, the liquid should be thickening. If not, raise the heat and cook another couple of minutes, stirring to prevent the vegetables from sticking. Add the remaining oil gradually, stirring vigorously with the back of a spoon as you do so.

Add the peas and asparagus to the skillet. Cook, stirring occasionally, for 3 minutes, or until the vegetables are brightly colored and just tender. Chop or slice the chicken and return it to the skillet, along with any juices that have accumulated. Add the lemon juice. Warm through, then taste and adjust the seasoning. Serve in shallow bowls, garnished with parsley.

NUTRITION PER SERVING: 445 calories, 41 g carbs, 7 g fiber, 25 g protein, 16 g total fat, 2 g saturated fat, 995 mg sodium

southern unfried chicken

Recipe by Art Smith

makes 4 servings

**total time: 1 hour 25 minutes
(plus marinating time)**

Art Smith—who owns restaurants in Atlanta, Washington, DC, and Chicago and was Oprah Winfrey's personal chef for 10 years—loves his southern comfort food. But after taking up running and losing 120 pounds, he knew his beloved high-fat dishes needed a healthy makeover. "When people think 'healthy,' they think of a salad," says Smith. "But that's not the only choice. It's easy to remake burgers, fried chicken, and burritos into meals that don't go over the top on calories." Now instead of frying battered chicken, Smith marinates it, coats it in a spicy whole wheat panko bread crumb mixture, and bakes it. It's a recipe he created for his health-minded restaurant Lyfe Kitchen in California. The result is a crispy, flavor-packed meal with a fraction of the fat of the original. Serve the chicken with Steel Cut Oatmeal Risotto with Asparagus (page 217) as a side.

---

1 cup buttermilk

2 to 3 teaspoons hot sauce

4 boneless, skinless chicken breasts, cut in half

1½ cups whole wheat panko bread crumbs

3 tablespoons freshly grated Parmesan cheese

1½ teaspoons onion powder

1½ teaspoons garlic powder

1 to 2 teaspoons ground black pepper

1 to 2 teaspoons cayenne pepper

1 teaspoon paprika

¼ teaspoon salt

In a bowl, combine the buttermilk and hot sauce. Submerge the chicken in the buttermilk marinade. Allow to marinate in the refrigerator for at least 1 hour and up to 24 hours.

Combine the bread crumbs, cheese, onion powder, garlic powder, black pepper, cayenne, paprika, and salt in a resealable plastic bag. Shake to blend.

Using tongs, remove the chicken from the marinade and place directly in the bag with the bread crumb mixture. Shake the bag well, until the chicken breasts are evenly coated.

Coat a sheet pan with cooking spray. Remove the chicken from the bag and place in a single layer on the pan. Chill, uncovered, in the refrigerator for 30 minutes.

Preheat the oven to 400°F. Lightly coat each chicken breast with cooking spray. Bake for 35 to 40 minutes, or until a thermometer inserted in the center of a piece of chicken reads 165°F.

NUTRITION PER SERVING: 311 calories, 25 g carbs, 4 g fiber, 38 g protein, 6 g total fat, 2 g saturated fat, 520 mg sodium

marinated grilled chicken

Recipe by Liz Applegate, PhD

makes 4 servings

total time: 35 minutes (plus marinating time)

Versatile, healthy, and budget-friendly, chicken is an ideal protein source for runners. But if it's not prepared the right way, it can turn out bland and tasteless. This easy grilled chicken recipe is anything but bland, thanks to the flavor-packed marinade made with rich soy sauce and lime juice. It's guaranteed to become a staple at your postrace summer cookouts. Make extra, and shred or cube the leftovers to use in salads and other dishes throughout the week. To speed recovery to tired muscles, serve the chicken with rice or pasta.

- ¼ **cup soy sauce**
- 1 **tablespoon lime juice**
- 3 **tablespoons extra-virgin olive oil**
- 1 **teaspoon fresh thyme or any fresh herb**
-   **Salt**
-   **Ground black pepper**
- 1½ **pounds skinless chicken pieces (breast, thigh, and drumsticks, with or without bone)**

In a small bowl, whisk together the soy sauce, lime juice, oil, and thyme. Season with salt and pepper.

Place the chicken in a resealable plastic bag. Pour the marinade over it. Seal the bag and gently turn it to coat the chicken. Put the chicken in the refrigerator and let it marinate for 1 to 6 hours.

Coat a grill rack with oil and preheat the grill. Place the chicken on the grill and cook over medium heat for 10 to 12 minutes per side for bone-in chicken and 6 minutes for boneless, or until a thermometer inserted in the center reads 165°F.

NUTRITION PER SERVING: 230 calories, 1 g carbs, 0 g fiber, 36 g protein, 9 g total fat, 2 g saturated fat, 720 mg sodium

chicken-mango fajitas

Recipe by Matthew Kadey, MS, RD

makes 4 servings

total time: 25 minutes

Lean chicken breast delivers plenty of muscle-friendly protein and energizing B vitamins, while mango adds a sweet kick and good amounts of vitamin C. Top with avocado for a creamy finish and a dose of heart-healthy monounsaturated fat.

1 teaspoon paprika

½ teaspoon garlic powder

½ teaspoon onion powder

½ teaspoon ground cumin

½ teaspoon salt

½ teaspoon ground black pepper

1 tablespoon canola oil

1 pound boneless, skinless chicken breast, cut into ½" slices

1 thinly sliced red bell pepper

1 thinly sliced yellow bell pepper

1 mango, peeled, seeded, and cubed

8 (6") flour tortillas, warmed

1 avocado, cubed

¼ cup sour cream (optional)

In a small bowl, combine the paprika, garlic powder, onion powder, cumin, salt, and pepper.

Heat a skillet over medium-high heat. Add the oil and chicken. Cook for 3 minutes, or until no longer pink. Remove the chicken from the skillet.

Add the red and yellow bell peppers. Cook for 2 minutes, stirring often. Return the chicken to the skillet along with the spice mixture and mango. Heat through for 1 minute.

Spoon the mixture onto the tortillas and top with the avocado and sour cream, if using.

NUTRITION PER SERVING: 353 calories, 32 g carbs, 7 g fiber, 28 g protein, 13 g total fat, 2 g saturated fat, 439 mg sodium

chicken stir-fry with green beans and broccoli

Recipe by Nate Appleman

makes 4 servings

total time: 40 minutes

Stir-frying is a speedy process, so you won't have time to chop and mix once you start cooking. Have your ingredients ready to go—cut the vegetables into small, nearly bite-size uniform pieces for even cooking. "This dish cooks in minutes," says Runner's World *contributing chef Nate Appleman, "and you can substitute ground turkey for the chicken." Sriracha, a widely available hot chili sauce, provides a spicy kick plus capsaicin, a compound that boosts fat burning during exercise. Serve the stir-fry with brown rice.*

- 2 tablespoons canola oil
- 1 pound ground chicken breast
- 1 small onion, thinly sliced
- 3 cloves garlic, minced
- 1 tablespoon peeled and grated fresh ginger
- ½ pound trimmed green beans, cut in half (about 3 cups loosely packed)
- ½ pound broccoli crowns, cut into ½" pieces (about 3 cups)
- ½ pound cabbage, thinly sliced (about 3 cups loosely packed)
- ¼ pound shiitake mushrooms, thinly sliced (about 1¼ cups loosely packed)
- 3 tablespoons reduced-sodium soy sauce
- 2 tablespoons sriracha or other hot chili sauce

- 1 tablespoon rice wine vinegar or lime juice
- 3 scallions (green and white parts), thinly sliced
- 1 bunch cilantro, stems removed, coarsely chopped
- ⅛ teaspoon salt, optional
- ¼ cup chopped peanuts

Heat a wok or large skillet over medium-high heat. Add 1 tablespoon of the oil. Add the chicken and cook for 5 minutes, or until no longer pink. Remove the chicken from the wok.

In the same pan, add the remaining 1 tablespoon oil and the onion. Cook for 2 to 3 minutes, or until the onion is translucent.

Add the garlic and ginger and cook for 1 minute, or until fragrant and golden, being careful not to let either burn.

Add the green beans, broccoli, cabbage, and mushrooms. Cook for 5 minutes, or until slightly tender.

Add the soy sauce, sriracha, and vinegar or lime juice. Cook for 2 to 3 minutes, or until reduced slightly.

Return the chicken to the wok. Add the scallions and cilantro. Remove the wok from the heat and add the salt, if using. Garnish with the peanuts.

NUTRITION PER SERVING: 318 calories, 23 g carbs, 7 g fiber, 33 g protein, 13 g total fat, 1 g saturated fat, 738 mg sodium

chicken with asparagus, mushrooms, and rice

Recipe by Liz Applegate, PhD

makes 4 servings

total time: 1 hour 20 minutes

This one-pot meal provides runner-friendly carbs and protein—with minimal cleanup. Juicy, flavorful chicken thighs contain slightly more fat than chicken breasts but also provide more iron and zinc, two minerals that many runners don't get enough of.

---

1 tablespoon extra-virgin olive oil

4 chicken thighs

1 small onion, chopped

2 cloves garlic, minced

4 ounces sliced mushrooms (about 2 cups)

1 cup brown rice

½ teaspoon salt

¼ teaspoon ground black pepper

½ teaspoon poultry seasoning

2 cups chicken broth

1½ cups asparagus, cut into 2" pieces

Heat a large pot or Dutch oven over medium heat. Add the oil and chicken. Brown the chicken for 5 minutes per side. Remove from the pot.

Add the onion to the same pot and cook, stirring frequently, for 5 minutes, or until it begins to soften. Add the garlic and cook, stirring frequently, for 1 minute. Add the mushrooms and cook, stirring frequently, for 3 minutes, or until they begin to soften.

Add the rice, salt, pepper, and poultry seasoning. Cook, stirring frequently, for 5 minutes, or until the rice begins to lightly toast. Add the broth and bring to a boil.

Return the chicken to the pot. Reduce the heat to low and simmer, covered, for 30 minutes. Add the asparagus. Simmer for 10 to 15 minutes, or until the liquid is absorbed and the rice is tender.

NUTRITION PER SERVING: 328 calories, 42 g carbs, 3 g fiber, 21 g protein, 9 g total fat, 2 g saturated fat, 857 mg sodium

red beans and rice with turkey sausage

Recipe by Nick Symmonds

makes 6 servings

total time: 55 minutes

"When I come back from a hard workout," says 800-meter Olympian Nick Symmonds, "my body is craving carbohydrates and protein." That's when he whips up a big pot of red beans and rice—comfort food that also satisfies his recovery needs and makes for great leftovers. If Symmonds feels like he needs an extra protein boost, he'll toss in lean smoked turkey sausage, which also punches up the flavor.

5 cups low-sodium chicken broth

2 cups brown rice

2 tablespoons extra-virgin olive oil

1 green bell pepper, chopped

1 red bell pepper, chopped

2 onions, chopped

2 cloves garlic, minced

1 pound smoked turkey sausage, cut into ½" slices

2 cans (15 ounces) kidney beans, drained and rinsed

1 can (14.5 ounces) diced tomatoes

1 teaspoon dried thyme

1 bay leaf

Ground black pepper

Hot sauce (optional)

In a medium pot, combine 4½ cups of the broth and the rice. Bring to a boil. Stir, cover, reduce the heat to low, and simmer for 40 minutes, or until the liquid is absorbed.

Meanwhile, heat the oil in a large pot over medium heat. Add the green and red bell peppers and onions. Cook, stirring frequently, for 5 minutes, or until softened. Add the garlic and cook for 1 minute.

Add the sausage and cook, stirring frequently, for 5 to 7 minutes, or until browned. Add the beans, tomatoes (with juice), thyme, bay leaf, and the remaining ½ cup broth. Simmer, uncovered, for 20 minutes, stirring occasionally. Season to taste with black pepper and hot sauce, if using. Remove the bay leaf.

Add the cooked rice to the bean and sausage mixture. Stir to combine and serve.

NUTRITION PER SERVING: 410 calories, 56 g carbs, 8 g fiber, 20 g protein, 11 g total fat, 3 g saturated fat, 907 mg sodium

Fish and Seafood Mains

grilled salmon with lentil tabbouleh

Recipe by Stefanie Sacks, MS, CNS, CDN

makes 6 servings

total time: 25 minutes

Lentils replace bulgur in this carb-, protein-, and fiber-rich tabbouleh, which serves as a base for the grilled salmon. When possible, splurge on wild Alaskan salmon. Not only is it fished in a sustainable way, but it's also loaded with inflammation-reducing omega-3 fatty acids. In addition, it has a healthier fat ratio—and richer flavor—than farmed salmon.

TABBOULEH

- **1 cup green or brown lentils**
- **3 cups water**
- **¼ cup extra-virgin olive oil**
- **½ cup lemon juice**
- **1 clove garlic, minced**
- **4 scallions, thinly sliced**
- **1 cup coarsely chopped flat-leaf parsley**
- **½ seedless cucumber, peeled and diced**
- **½ pint grape tomatoes, quartered**
- **1 teaspoon salt, plus more as needed**

SALMON

- **6 salmon fillets (4 ounces each)**
- **Juice of 1 lemon**
- **½ teaspoon salt**
- **3 teaspoons extra-virgin olive oil**

TO MAKE THE TABBOULEH: In a small pot, combine the lentils and water. Cover, raise the heat to high, and bring to a boil. Reduce the heat to low and simmer, covered, for 15 minutes, or until tender.

Meanwhile, in a bowl, toss together the oil, lemon juice, garlic, scallions, parsley, cucumber, tomatoes, and salt. When the lentils are cooked, drain, then add to the bowl and toss to combine. Taste and adjust the seasoning.

TO MAKE THE SALMON: Rinse the salmon under cold water, then pat dry with a paper towel. Squeeze the lemon juice over the flesh side, then season with the salt.

Brush the salmon with 2 teaspoons of the oil. Heat a grill pan on medium-high heat and add the remaining 1 teaspoon oil. When hot, cook the salmon, skin side down, for 4 minutes, or until the skin is crispy and releases easily from the pan. Flip and cook for 2 to 3 minutes, or until the fish is just cooked through. Spritz with any remaining lemon juice. Serve the salmon over the tabbouleh.

NUTRITION PER SERVING: 412 calories, 25 g carbs, 11 g fiber, 34 g protein, 20 g total fat, 3 g saturated fat, 661 mg sodium

mini salmon cakes with salsa

Recipe by Matthew Kadey, MS, RD

makes 4 servings

total time: 30 minutes

While fresh wild salmon can be pricey, the canned version is a fraction of the cost. And it has the added convenience of being precooked and shelf stable, so you can stock your pantry for quick meals like this one any night of the week. Like fresh salmon, canned wild salmon is a rich source of DHA, a type of omega-3 fat that promotes brain health and helps lower blood triglycerides, reducing heart disease risk.

---

2 cans (6 ounces each) wild salmon, drained and flaked

1 cup frozen chopped spinach, thawed and squeezed dry

1 red bell pepper, cut into small dice

2 tablespoons chopped fresh dill

Juice of ½ lemon

½ cup quick-cooking rolled oats

2 eggs

Salt and ground black pepper

½ cup fresh salsa

Preheat the oven to 375°F. Lightly coat 12 muffin cups with cooking spray.

In a large bowl, combine the salmon, spinach, bell pepper, dill, lemon juice, oats, and eggs. Season to taste with salt and pepper. Stir until well combined.

Divide the mixture among the muffin cups. Bake for 20 minutes. Let the salmon cakes cool before removing them from the cups. Serve topped with the salsa.

NUTRITION PER SERVING: 188 calories, 13 g carbs, 3 g fiber, 22 g protein, 6 g total fat, 1 g saturated fat, 493 mg sodium

salmon coconut curry

Recipe by Matthew Kadey, MS, RD

makes 4 servings

total time: 40 minutes

This simple, delicious curry combines the potent flavor of a savory spice blend with the creaminess of coconut milk, cut with a hint of refreshing lime. It's perfect after a tough run, when your body needs the inflammation-reducing antioxidants found in curry powder, along with the protein and carbohydrates in salmon and sweet potatoes.

- 2 teaspoons canola oil
- 2 shallots, chopped
- 2 cloves garlic, minced
- 2 cups chicken broth
- 1 can (13.5 ounces) light coconut milk
- 2 sweet potatoes, cubed
- 2 tablespoons tomato paste
- 1 tablespoon peeled and minced fresh ginger
- 1 tablespoon curry powder
- 1 teaspoon ground cumin
- ¼ teaspoon cayenne pepper
- ¼ teaspoon salt
- ¼ teaspoon ground black pepper
- 1 pound skinless salmon, cut into 1" cubes
- 1½ cups frozen peas
- Juice of 1 lime
- Fresh cilantro

Heat the oil in a large pot over medium heat. Add the shallots and garlic. Cook, stirring frequently, for 2 minutes.

Add the broth, coconut milk, sweet potatoes, tomato paste, ginger, curry, cumin, cayenne, salt, and black pepper. Raise the heat to high and bring to a boil. Reduce the heat to low and simmer for 20 minutes.

Add the salmon. Simmer for 4 minutes, or until just underdone. Add the peas and lime juice, and simmer for 3 minutes, or until just heated through. Garnish with the cilantro.

NUTRITION PER SERVING: 395 calories, 32 g carbs, 5 g fiber, 32 g protein, 15 g total fat, 6.5 g saturated fat, 853 mg sodium

spicy fish tacos with pineapple slaw

Recipe by Nate Appleman

makes 4 servings

total time: 55 minutes (including marinating time)

Grilling—rather than frying—the fish keeps these tacos healthful while providing plenty of lean protein. The sour cream and chile marinade gives the fish a rich, spicy flavor that's balanced by the cool, slightly sweet slaw. If you prefer milder spice, use one-quarter of the canned peppers. Using half the can will give you a medium spice level. Look for canned chipotle peppers in adobo sauce in the Latin food aisle at any grocery store.

- 1 can (7 ounces) chipotle chiles in adobo sauce (wear plastic gloves when handling)
- ½ cup sour cream
- 1 tablespoon extra-virgin olive oil, plus more for the grill
- ¾ cup chopped cilantro Salt
- 1 pound skinless, firm-fleshed fish, such as mahi mahi, tilapia, Pacific halibut, or catfish
- 4 cups thinly shredded green cabbage
- ½ small red onion, thinly sliced
- ½ jalapeño chile, seeded and minced (wear plastic gloves when handling)
- ½ cup diced pineapple Juice of 1 lime
- ½ teaspoon ground cumin
- ½ teaspoon dried oregano
- 1 avocado, sliced
- 8 small (6") corn tortillas

Chop one-quarter to one-half of the chipotle chiles and place in a small bowl, along with any adobo sauce that clings to them. Add the sour cream, oil, and ½ cup of the cilantro. Season with salt and stir to combine. Reserve ¼ cup of the marinade.

Place the fish on a plate and spread the remaining marinade over both sides of it. Let it sit for at least 30 minutes.

In a large bowl, mix together the cabbage, onion, jalapeño pepper, pineapple, lime juice, cumin, oregano, and the remaining ¼ cup cilantro. Stir to combine and season to taste with salt.

Sprinkle the avocado slices with salt.

Coat a grill rack with oil and preheat the grill. Remove the fish from the marinade (discarding whatever marinade remains in the dish) and grill over medium heat, turning once, for 6 to 8 minutes, or until nicely charred and cooked through. Alternatively, place an oven rack closest to the heat source and turn on the broiler. Coat a baking pan with cooking spray, place the fish on the pan, and broil for 6 to 8 minutes. Remove the fish to a cutting board and coarsely chop.

Place the tortillas on a baking sheet and toast under the broiler for 1 minute. Lay out the tortillas and divide the fish among them. Top with the cabbage slaw and avocado. Spoon the reserved marinade over the tacos.

NUTRITION PER SERVING: 394 calories, 42 g carbs, 7 g fiber, 26 g protein, 15 g total fat, 3.5 g saturated fat, 504 mg sodium

barramundi in saffron broth

Recipe by Matthew Kadey, MS, RD

makes 4 servings

total time: 15 minutes

Many runners may not be familiar with barramundi, but it's well worth putting this newcomer on the menu. Native to Australia, barramundi is farmed in an environmentally sound way in the United States. It has a firm, moist texture and sweet flavor that's not at all fishy. Five ounces provide 27 grams of protein and 833 milligrams of omega-3s—nearly three times as much as cod and tilapia. If your grocer doesn't sell it fresh, check the freezer aisle. Frozen fillets retain their texture and flavor.

- 1 tablespoon canola oil
- 20 ounces barramundi or striped bass, cut into 4 fillets
- 1½ cups chicken broth
- ½ teaspoon saffron
- 1 teaspoon chopped fresh dill

Heat the oil in a large skillet over medium heat. Add the fish and cook for 2 minutes per side. Remove the fish from the skillet.

Add the broth and saffron to the skillet. Bring the broth to a simmer, then return the fillets to the pan and cook for 2 minutes, or until they are cooked through (they will be white opaque throughout) and flake easily.

Divide the broth and fish among 4 bowls. Top with the dill. Serve with a slice of crusty bread.

NUTRITION PER SERVING: 175 calories, 0 g carbs, 0 g fiber, 27 g protein, 6 g total fat, 1 g saturated fat, 242 mg sodium

maple-glazed arctic char

Recipe by Matthew Kadey, MS, RD

makes 4 servings

total time: 20 minutes

With its pink hue, arctic char resembles salmon but has a milder flavor similar to trout. Like salmon, it's a good source of DHA and EPA, omega-3s that protect against heart disease. The pink coloring comes from an antioxidant called astaxanthin, which may help raise HDL, or so-called "good cholesterol." Most char available in the United States is farmed in land-based, closed tanks, so there's little risk that pollutants or fish can escape into open water. Brushing the fillets with a maple syrup glaze brings out the fish's natural sweetness. Serve on a bed of steamed or lightly sautéed greens.

1½ **pounds arctic char (or salmon or trout), cut into 4 fillets**

2 **tablespoons maple syrup**

1 **tablespoon balsamic vinegar**

1 **tablespoon orange zest**

Preheat the oven to 450°F. Lightly coat a glass baking dish with cooking spray. Place the fish fillets in the dish (skin side down if still attached).

In a small bowl, stir together the maple syrup, vinegar, and orange zest. Brush the mixture on top of the fish. Bake for 12 to 15 minutes, or until the fish flakes easily with a fork, brushing the fish with the glaze again halfway through.

NUTRITION PER SERVING: 293 calories, 8 g carbs, 0 g fiber, 34 g protein, 14 g total fat, 0 g saturated fat, 89 mg sodium

sablefish with pomegranate syrup

Recipe by Matthew Kadey, MS, RD

makes 4 servings

total time: 20 minutes

Sablefish goes by many names, including black cod (in reference to its dark skin) and butterfish, after its nearly melt-in-your mouth texture—the result of a high omega-3 fatty acid content. In fact, 6 ounces of sablefish has 2,800 milligrams of omega-3s, about 30 percent more than wild salmon. This also means the fish won't dry out quickly, making it ideal for high-heat cooking, like broiling. Look for wild-caught sablefish from Alaska and the Canadian Pacific for the most environmentally friendly choice.

---

1 cup pomegranate juice

1 tablespoon packed brown sugar

1 tablespoon balsamic vinegar

4 fillets sablefish (or salmon), 6 ounces each

Salt and ground black pepper

In a small saucepan over high heat, combine the pomegranate juice, brown sugar, and vinegar. Bring to a boil, then reduce the heat and simmer for 12 minutes, or until the mixture turns into a syrup.

Meanwhile, place an oven rack 4" to 5" from the heat source and turn on the broiler. Lightly coat a baking pan with cooking spray. Place the fish on the pan and lightly season with salt and pepper. Broil for 8 to 10 minutes, or until opaque in the center. Remove the fish from the oven and brush with the pomegranate syrup.

NUTRITION PER SERVING: 383 calories, 13 g carbs, 0 g fiber, 23 g protein, 26 g total fat, 5.5 g saturated fat, 250 mg sodium

pacific halibut with kiwi salsa

Recipe by Matthew Kadey, MS, RD

makes 4 servings

total time: 20 minutes

Pacific halibut has a mild flavor and meaty texture that will appeal to even fussy seafood eaters. It's virtually free of saturated fat and provides protein, omega-3s, selenium, potassium, and vitamin B$_6$. Halibut from Alaska, Washington, and Oregon fisheries are the most sustainable. Avoid Atlantic halibut, which has been overfished, reducing populations to extremely low levels. Because it's a leaner fish, Pacific halibut can quickly dry out. Cooking it with moist heat, like this poaching method, keeps the fish tender.

3½ **cups chicken broth**

Juice of 2 lemons

1 **tablespoon black peppercorns**

4 **sprigs fresh thyme**

4 **fillets Pacific halibut (or Pacific flounder), 6 ounces each**

2 **kiwi, diced**

1 **jalapeño chile pepper, seeded and diced (wear plastic gloves when handling)**

Juice of ½ lime

1 **tablespoon chopped fresh cilantro**

In a large saucepan over high heat, combine the broth, lemon juice, peppercorns, and thyme. Bring to a boil. Turn off the heat, add the fish, cover, and let stand for 10 minutes, until the fish is cooked through.

Meanwhile, in a small bowl, combine the kiwi, chile pepper, lime juice, and cilantro. Stir to blend the flavors.

When the fish is done, remove it from the saucepan and serve topped with the kiwi salsa.

NUTRITION PER SERVING: 232 calories, 9 g carbs, 2 g fiber, 39 g protein, 4 g total fat, 0.5 g saturated fat, 593 mg sodium

sweet and sour shrimp stir-fry

Recipe by Matthew Kadey, MS, RD

makes 4 servings

total time: 15 minutes

Not only is shrimp a lean source of protein, but it also provides the mineral selenium, which may help reduce joint inflammation that runners can experience from training. Using frozen vegetables helps get this meal on the table fast. If you're not a fan of lima beans, you can use frozen edamame or fava beans instead. Serve the stir-fry with brown rice.

- 1 tablespoon canola oil
- 2 teaspoons minced garlic
- 1 teaspoon red-pepper flakes
- 1 package (12 ounces) frozen Asian vegetable medley
- 1 cup frozen lima beans
- 1 pound frozen cooked shrimp
- 1 cup unsalted cashews
- 1 can (20 ounces) pineapple chunks, juice reserved
- 1 jar (10 ounces) store-bought sweet and sour sauce

Heat the oil in a large skillet over medium heat. Add the garlic, pepper flakes, vegetable medley, and lima beans. Cook for 5 minutes, stirring frequently.

Stir in the frozen shrimp and cook for 3 minutes. Add the cashews, pineapple, ⅓ cup of the pineapple juice, and the sweet and sour sauce. Heat through for 2 minutes.

NUTRITION PER SERVING: 665 calories, 77 g carbs, 7 g fiber, 40 g protein, 23 g total fat, 3.5 g saturated fat, 785 mg sodium

garlic shrimp with white beans and tomatoes

Recipe by Pam Anderson

makes 4 servings

total time: 20 minutes

Runner's World *contributing chef Pam Anderson whips up this protein-packed skillet dish for an easy postrun weeknight dinner. If you use frozen shrimp, save the liquid from thawing and swap it for some of the chicken broth. Pimenton, or smoked paprika, adds a uniquely rich and smokey flavor. If you don't already own a bottle, it's worth adding this spice to your pantry.*

1 pound shrimp, peeled and deveined

4 tablespoons extra-virgin olive oil

1 teaspoon pimenton (smoked paprika)

3 cloves garlic, minced

½ teaspoon red-pepper flakes

1 bay leaf, broken into pieces

1 can (14.5 ounces) petite-diced tomatoes, drained

1 tablespoon tomato paste

2 cans (15 ounces each) white beans, drained and rinsed

1 cup chicken broth

2 tablespoons chopped fresh parsley

Heat a large skillet over medium-high heat. In a bowl, toss the shrimp with 1 tablespoon of the oil and the pimenton. Add the shrimp to the skillet and cook, stirring frequently, for 1 to 2 minutes, or until golden pink and just cooked through. Add half of the garlic during the last few seconds of cooking. Spoon the shrimp into a bowl.

Return the skillet to the heat. Add 2 tablespoons of the oil, the pepper flakes, bay leaf, and the remaining garlic. Cook for just a few seconds, or until the garlic is fragrant and turns golden. Add the tomatoes and cook for 2 minutes, or until most of the liquid evaporates.

Add the tomato paste and cook until the mixture starts to darken. Add the beans and broth. Simmer for 4 to 5 minutes, or until it reaches a thick stew consistency. Stir in the shrimp and parsley. Continue cooking for 1 to 2 minutes, or until just heated through. Drizzle with the remaining 1 tablespoon oil. Serve immediately.

NUTRITION PER SERVING: 436 calories, 37 g carbs, 9 g fiber, 35 g protein, 17 g total fat, 2.5 g saturated fat, 412 mg sodium

jerk shrimp with sweet potato and black beans

Recipe by Matthew Kadey, MS, RD

makes 4 servings

total time: 25 minutes

This Caribbean-inspired dish uses jerk seasoning, which is made from a variety of spices including allspice, cloves, cinnamon, thyme, and plenty of hot peppers. It provides a flavor punch while adding very few calories. When possible, look for US farmed or wild shrimp, which is more sustainable than imported.

- **1 pound shrimp, peeled and deveined**
- **2 tablespoons jerk seasoning**
- **1 tablespoon canola oil**
- **1 sweet potato, thinly sliced**
- **1 can (15 ounces) black beans, drained and rinsed**
- **3 cloves garlic, sliced**
- **1 jalapeño chile, seeded and minced (wear plastic gloves when handling)**
- **2 scallions, sliced**
- **¼ cup orange juice**
- **Chopped fresh cilantro**

In a large bowl, toss together the shrimp and jerk seasoning.

Heat a wok or skillet over medium-high heat. Add the oil. When hot, add the shrimp. Cook, stirring, for 3 minutes, or until they turn pink. Remove from the wok.

Add the sweet potato to the wok and cook for 4 minutes, or until tender. Stir in the beans, garlic, chile pepper, and scallions. Cook, stirring constantly, for 1 minute.

Stir in the shrimp and orange juice. Heat for 30 seconds. Serve garnished with the cilantro.

NUTRITION PER SERVING: 229 calories, 20 g carbs, 4 g fiber, 24 g protein, 5 g total fat, 0.5 g saturated fat, 662 mg sodium

crab and black bean tacos

Recipe by Matthew Kadey, MS, RD

makes 6 servings

total time: 20 minutes

Canned crabmeat is a great way to reel in muscle-friendly protein, bone-building phosphorus, and zinc. Just 3 ounces provide nearly a quarter of your daily need for zinc, which is key for immune function. The best brands of lump or white crabmeat will have a firm texture, clean and light flavor, and no fishy scent. To make this gluten-free, just swap in corn tortillas for the flour ones.

½ cup low-fat plain yogurt

1 teaspoon curry powder

⅛ teaspoon cayenne pepper

12 ounces canned crabmeat, picked through

1 can (15 ounces) black beans, drained and rinsed

1 mango, peeled, pitted, and cut into bite-size cubes

1 to 2 tablespoons lime juice

¼ teaspoon salt

12 small (6") flour tortillas

2 cups arugula or baby spinach

In a small bowl, whisk together the yogurt, curry powder, and cayenne.

In a medium bowl, stir together the crabmeat, beans, mango, lime juice, and salt.

Heat the tortillas according to the package directions. Divide the crab mixture among the tortillas. Top with a dollop of the curry yogurt and the arugula or spinach. Fold up the sides and eat taco-style.

NUTRITION PER SERVING: 344 calories, 50 g carbs, 5 g fiber, 22 g protein, 6 g total fat, 1.5 g saturated fat, 776 mg sodium

crab-and-lentil-stuffed tomato with yogurt sauce

Recipe by Matthew Kadey, MS, RD

makes 6 servings

total time: 20 minutes

This variation on stuffed peppers uses scooped-out fresh tomatoes to hold a carb- and protein-packed filling. Unlike traditional stuffed peppers, this version doesn't require any cooking, making it ideal after a summer run when you don't feel like standing in front of a hot stove.

12 ounces canned crabmeat, picked through

1 cup canned lentils

2 ribs celery, sliced

2 scallions, sliced

¼ cup pine nuts

2 tablespoons chopped fresh basil or oregano

Juice of 1 lemon

Salt and ground black pepper

½ cup low-fat plain Greek yogurt

1 teaspoon crab-boil seasoning

6 large tomatoes

In a medium bowl, combine the crabmeat, lentils, celery, scallions, pine nuts, basil or oregano, and half of the lemon juice. Season to taste with salt and pepper.

In a small bowl, whisk together the yogurt, crab-boil seasoning, and the remaining lemon juice.

Slice off the tops of the tomatoes. Guide a knife around the inside. Scoop out the innards and discard and fill the tomato with the crab mixture. Top with the yogurt sauce.

NUTRITION PER SERVING: 181 calories, 13 g carbs, 5 g fiber, 18 g protein, 7 g total fat, 2 g saturated fat, 401 mg sodium

coconut-lime mussels

Recipe by Matthew Kadey, MS, RD

makes 4 servings

total time: 15 minutes

Inexpensive, tasty, and easy to prepare, mussels are a good source of omega-3 fatty acids, iron, vitamin B$_{12}$, and protein, containing 20 grams in just 3 ounces. When buying mussels, make sure their shells are tightly closed and avoid any that are cracked. They're best when cooked the same day you purchase them. Store in the refrigerator in a bowl covered loosely with a damp paper towel until you're ready to use them.

2 pounds mussels

1 can (13.5 ounces) light coconut milk

Juice of 2 limes

½ cup fresh cilantro, coarsely chopped

½ teaspoon red-pepper flakes

Put the mussels in a large colander set in the sink. Rinse with cool water. Sort through them and discard any mussels that have cracked shells. Pull off any mosslike growth where the shells close. (This is called the beard. However, most farmed mussels are debearded before being sold, so you may be able to skip this step.)

In a large saucepan over high heat, combine the coconut milk, lime juice, cilantro, and pepper flakes. Bring to a boil. Add the mussels, cover, reduce the heat to medium, and simmer for 3 minutes, or until they open. Discard any that stay shut. Serve the mussels with the coconut sauce for dipping.

NUTRITION PER SERVING: 265 calories, 10 g carbs, 0 g fiber, 28 g protein, 11 g total fat, 6 g saturated fat, 669 mg sodium

9

Vegetables

Vegetarian Mains

Vegetable Sides

brown rice salad with curried tofu

Recipe by Melissa Lasher

makes 4 servings

total time: 45 minutes

Opting for brown rice over white makes this dish a nutritional knockout. While the two contain an identical amount of carbs, brown rice contains four times as much insoluble fiber and magnesium. A deficit in the latter can hinder endurance. This whole grain meal gets plenty of staying power from the protein in tofu and the healthy fats in seeds. Try making this for dinner the night before a long run for energy that lasts. To make sure you always have brown rice on hand (and to save on prep time), cook up a batch and store it in small quantities in the freezer.

- 1 cup brown rice
- 1 package (14 ounces) extra-firm tofu, cut into ½" cubes
- 2 tablespoons extra-virgin olive oil
- 1 teaspoon curry powder
- 1 teaspoon salt
- ½ cup shredded coconut
- 1½ cups frozen edamame, thawed
- ½ cup sunflower seeds
- ½ cup toasted pumpkin seeds
- 1 cup halved cherry tomatoes
- 2 grinds of black pepper

Cook the rice according to package directions. Preheat the oven to 350°F.

In a large bowl, toss together the tofu, 1 tablespoon of the oil, ½ teaspoon of the curry powder, ½ teaspoon of the salt, and the coconut. Transfer to a baking sheet and bake for 15 minutes.

Meanwhile, in a large bowl, whisk together the remaining 1 tablespoon oil, ½ teaspoon curry powder, and ½ teaspoon salt. When the rice is cooked, add it to the bowl, followed by the edamame, sunflower seeds, pumpkin seeds, cherry tomatoes, and black pepper. Stir to combine, then gently stir in the cooked tofu.

NUTRITION PER SERVING: 551 calories, 54 g carbs, 9 g fiber, 23 g protein, 29 g total fat, 6 g saturated fat, 863 mg sodium

sweet and sour tofu stir-fry

Recipe by Matthew Kadey, MS, RD

makes 4 servings

total time: 45 minutes

Protein-rich tofu and carb-dense brown rice make this stir-fry ideal for repairing muscle and restocking energy stores after a run. Ginger adds an extra recovery punch—research shows it contains compounds that may ease postworkout muscle pain by dampening inflammation. While runners need to replenish lost sodium after a sweaty run, using low-sodium soy sauce and vegetable broth will help keep your salt intake in check and rebalance electrolyte levels.

1 cup brown rice

⅓ cup low-sodium vegetable broth

2 tablespoons rice vinegar

2 tablespoons ketchup

1 tablespoon low-sodium soy sauce

1 tablespoon packed brown sugar

2 teaspoons cornstarch

1 tablespoon canola oil

1 package (14 ounces) firm tofu, cut into ½" cubes

1 red bell pepper, sliced

2 cups broccoli florets

3 scallions, sliced

2 cloves garlic, sliced

1 tablespoon peeled and sliced fresh ginger

1 cup pineapple chunks

Cook the rice according to package directions.

Meanwhile, in a small bowl, whisk together the broth, vinegar, ketchup, soy sauce, brown sugar, and cornstarch.

Heat the oil in a wok or large skillet over medium-high heat. Add the tofu and cook for 4 minutes, or until the tofu is browned. Transfer it to a plate.

Add the bell pepper, broccoli, scallions, garlic, and ginger to the wok. Cook, stirring constantly, for 1 minute, or until the peppers are tender.

Add the tofu, pineapple, and broth mixture to the wok. Cook for 1 minute. Serve over the brown rice.

NUTRITION PER SERVING: 434 calories, 61 g carbs, 7 g fiber, 22 g protein, 14 g total fat, 2 g saturated fat, 253 mg sodium

chickpea and spinach stir-fry

Recipe by Matthew Kadey, MS, RD

makes 4 servings

total time: 15 minutes

Inexpensive chickpeas, a staple in Indian cuisine, are loaded with a range of vital nutrients, including B vitamins, iron, magnesium, protein, carbs, and fiber (providing 6 grams per half cup). Leafy greens like spinach are one of the richest sources of dietary nitrates, compounds that may help muscles work more efficiently during exercise. Garam masala is a blend of ground spices commonly used in Indian cooking. It often includes black pepper, cinnamon, cloves, coriander, cumin, and other spices. Look for it in the spice aisle at any grocery store.

- 1 tablespoon canola oil
- 2 cans (14 ounces each) chickpeas, drained and rinsed
- 3 cloves garlic, sliced
- 1 tablespoon peeled and chopped fresh ginger
- 1 tablespoon garam masala
- ½ teaspoon ground turmeric
- ¼ teaspoon cayenne pepper
- ¼ teaspoon salt
- 1 bunch fresh spinach, chopped (about 6 cups)
- 1 pint cherry tomatoes, halved
- Juice of ½ lemon
- Low-fat plain yogurt (omit for a vegan meal)

Heat the oil in a wok or large skillet over medium-high heat. Add the chickpeas, garlic, and ginger. Cook, stirring frequently, for 4 minutes.

Add the garam masala, turmeric, cayenne, and salt. Cook for 1 minute, stirring to blend.

Stir in the spinach and heat until it's wilted. Stir in the tomatoes and lemon juice. Heat for 30 seconds. Serve topped with a dollop of yogurt, if using.

NUTRITION PER SERVING: 228 calories, 37 g carbs, 9 g fiber, 10 g protein, 6 g total fat, 0.5 g saturated fat, 600 mg sodium

chickpea spread for bruschetta

Recipe by Nate Appleman

makes 10 servings

total time: 40 minutes

Runner's World *contributing chef Nate Appleman enjoys this spread— similar to a chunky hummus—for lunch, but it's equally tasty at breakfast or as a snack. He eats it as is on toasted bread or sometimes tops it with avocado and tomato. For a nonvegan version, he eats it with a fried or poached egg or 1 tablespoon of goat cheese. For a nonvegetarian version, he adds tuna and arugula. The recipe makes plenty, so store extra in the fridge to eat throughout the week.*

- 1 tablespoon extra-virgin olive oil, plus more to drizzle
- 1 clove garlic, minced
- 1 red onion, diced small
- 1 carrot, diced small
- 1 rib celery, diced small
- 1 teaspoon red-pepper flakes
- ½ cup white wine
- 1 can (15 ounces) chickpeas, drained and rinsed
- 1 bunch spinach
- ¼ cup water, plus more if needed
- ½ bunch parsley, coarsely chopped
- 1 loaf country bread

Heat the olive oil over medium heat in a large skillet. Add the garlic, onion, carrot, celery, and pepper flakes. Cook for 4 minutes, or until softened and translucent. Deglaze the skillet with the wine and reduce completely.

Add the chickpeas, spinach, and water. Cook for 20 minutes, adding more water if the pan gets too dry. In the last few minutes of cooking, stir in the parsley. Coarsely mash the mixture with a potato masher and remove from the heat.

Cut the bread into 10 slices, drizzle with the oil, and toast on a grill or under the broiler until nicely charred.

Spread the chickpea mixture on the bread. Enjoy as is or with any of the toppings mentioned above.

NUTRITION PER SERVING: 184 calories, 29 g carbs, 4 g fiber, 6 g protein, 4 g total fat, 0.5 g saturated fat, 363 mg sodium

dal with cauliflower, eggplant, and zucchini

Recipe by Mark Bittman

makes 4 servings

total time: 1 hour

After a long run in chilly weather, Runner's World *contributing food writer Mark Bittman savors every bite of this Indian lentil stew. The recipe is flexible enough to accommodate whatever vegetables you have on hand. Using cardamom pods, mustard seeds, and whole cloves infuses the dish with richly spiced flavor. If you don't have them on hand, try the streamlined variation for Quickest Dal with Cauliflower, Eggplant, and Zucchini instead (below).*

- 1 tablespoon vegetable oil, plus more as needed
- 1 tablespoon butter
- 1 cup chopped onion
- 2 tablespoons peeled and minced fresh ginger
- 1 tablespoon minced garlic
- 2 cups cauliflower florets and stems cut into bite-size pieces
- 1 cup cubed eggplant, salted, rinsed, and dried
- 1 cup cubed zucchini
- 4 cardamom pods
- 1 tablespoon mustard seeds
- 2 whole cloves
- Ground black pepper
- 1 dried mild chile, like ancho (optional)
- 1 cup brown or red lentils, washed and picked over
- Water
- Salt
- ½ cup chopped fresh cilantro

Combine the oil and butter in a large pot or Dutch oven over medium heat. When the butter is melted, add the onion, ginger, and garlic and cook, stirring, for 5 minutes, or until softened. Remove from the pot.

Raise the heat to medium-high. Add the cauliflower and cook, stirring, for 5 to 10 minutes, or until browned. Remove the cauliflower and add a little more oil to the pan to prevent sticking. Add the eggplant and zucchini and cook, stirring, for 5 to 10 minutes, or until browned. Add the cardamom, mustard seeds, cloves, black pepper (to taste), and the chile pepper, if using. Stir for 1 or 2 minutes, or until the spices are fragrant but not burning.

Return the onion mixture and the cauliflower to the pot. Add the lentils and enough water to cover by about 1". Bring to a boil, then adjust the heat so the mixture bubbles gently. Cover and cook, stirring occasionally and adding water if necessary (the mixture should be saucy but not soupy), for 25 to 35 minutes, or until the lentils are tender. (The recipe can be made ahead to this point. Refrigerate for up to a couple of days or freeze for months, and gently reheat before proceeding.) Remove the cardamom pods, cloves, and chile pepper. Sprinkle with salt, then taste and adjust the seasoning. Garnish with the cilantro and serve.

Quickest Dal with Cauliflower, Eggplant, and Zucchini
Omit the cardamom, mustard seeds, and cloves, and substitute 2 tablespoons curry powder, chaat masala, or garam masala. In the first step, put the oil, butter, vegetables, lentils, and seasoning in the pot at the same time and cover with water by about 2". Cook for 25 to 35 minutes, or until the lentils and vegetables are tender. Season to taste with salt and pepper. Garnish and serve.

NUTRITION PER SERVING: 281 calories, 39 g carbs, 18 g fiber, 15 g protein, 8 g total fat, 2.5 g saturated fat, 191 mg sodium

steel cut oatmeal risotto with asparagus

Recipe by Art Smith

makes 4 servings

total time: 30 minutes

Since losing 120 pounds through running and a healthy diet, chef Art Smith, of Lyfe Kitchen in California, tries to add vegetables to every meal—and asparagus is one of his favorites. Here he adds it to a whole grain risotto made with oats instead of traditional Arborio rice, a refined grain with less fiber. "I love risotto," says Smith, "and making it with steel cut oats makes it extra healthy and delicious." Try sprinkling the finished risotto with a little Parmesan cheese for extra flavor.

1½ **teaspoons extra-virgin olive oil**

1 **cup steel cut oats**

1 **onion, chopped**

2 **cloves garlic, minced**

2 **cups sliced asparagus (1" pieces)**

1 **cup sliced mushrooms (3 ounces)**

4 to 6 **cups vegetable broth, heated**

Salt and ground black pepper

2 **tablespoons chopped fresh flat-leaf parsley**

Heat the oil in a large skillet over medium heat. Add the oats. Cook, stirring frequently, for 3 to 4 minutes, or until just starting to take on color.

Add the onion, garlic, asparagus, and mushrooms. Stir briefly to combine.

Stir in ¼ cup of broth at a time until it is absorbed by the oats. Continue adding broth for 20 minutes, or until the oats are creamy and al dente. Season to taste with salt and pepper. Garnish with the parsley.

NUTRITION PER SERVING: 217 calories, 38 g carbs, 6 g fiber, 9 g protein, 5 g total fat, 1 g saturated fat, 623 mg sodium

grilled vegetable polenta casserole

Recipe by Deena Kastor

makes 10 servings

total time: 1 hour 30 minutes

One of the many highlights of summer is the variety and bounty of fresh vegetables that flood local farmers' markets. This recipe puts all those vitamin- and flavor-packed vegetables to good use in a delicious casserole created by Olympic bronze medalist Deena Kastor. Don't feel restricted to the vegetables mentioned here—use whatever tempts you at the market or what you have in your fridge. Kastor likes to make this dish for weekend get-togethers with friends, and she serves it with a fresh salad and crusty bread. To save time, you can use two 16-ounce tubes of premade polenta cut into ¼" slices, instead of making your own.

- **1 large eggplant, sliced lengthwise, ½" thick**
- **2 yellow squash, sliced lengthwise, ¼" thick**
- **4 portobello mushrooms**
- **1 bunch asparagus**
- **2 tablespoons extra-virgin olive oil**
- **8 cups water**
- **1 teaspoon salt**
- **2 cups polenta or coarse cornmeal**
- **1½ cups marinara sauce**
- **½ cup goat cheese, crumbled**
- **¼ cup coarsely chopped fresh basil**

Preheat a grill. Brush the eggplant, squash, mushrooms, and asparagus with the oil. Place the vegetables on the grill and cook over medium-high heat, turning the squash, mushrooms, and asparagus over after 4 minutes, and the eggplant after 5 or 6 minutes. Cook all the vegetables 4 minutes longer. Remove the vegetables from the grill. Slice each mushroom into 8 strips.

In a large pot over high heat, combine the water and salt and bring to a boil. Whisk in the polenta or cornmeal in a slow, steady stream. Reduce the heat to low and cook, stirring, for 20 to 30 minutes, or until the polenta reaches a thick but spreadable consistency.

Preheat the oven to 375°F. To assemble the casserole, put ½ cup of the marinara sauce on the bottom of a 13" x 9" baking dish. Add half of the polenta. Layer each of the grilled vegetables atop one another. Evenly spread the remaining polenta on top of the vegetables. Smother the top with the remaining marinara sauce. Sprinkle with the cheese and basil.

Cover with foil and bake for 30 minutes, or until the sauce starts to bubble. Remove the foil and bake for 10 minutes longer, or until the cheese browns. Let the casserole cool for 5 minutes before cutting.

NUTRITION PER SERVING: 254 calories, 36 g carbs, 6 g fiber, 10 g protein, 9 g total fat, 3 g saturated fat, 596 mg sodium

mushroom tacos al pastor

Recipe by Lydia Maruniak

makes 2 servings

total time: 25 minutes

These vegetarian tacos have the rich flavor and meaty texture of tacos al pastor, a traditional Mexican dish that features chile-marinated, slow-cooked pork. But unlike the meat version, mushrooms only take about 10 minutes or so to cook on the stove. Plus, they're nearly fat-free and are a good source of B vitamins. It's a fast and filling recipe that's supereasy to make for a large crowd. For a sweet kick, try the tacos topped with fresh or roasted pineapple, a traditional pairing. Leave out the queso fresco to keep this recipe vegan.

---

3 tablespoons extra-virgin olive oil

1 yellow onion, diced

1 pound assorted mushrooms (such as creminis and portobellos), cleaned and cut into large chunks

2 cloves garlic, minced

1 teaspoon ground cumin

1 teaspoon dried oregano

2 teaspoons chili powder (use dark chili powder if you like a bit more heat)

1 orange, juiced

1 lime, juiced, plus 2 wedges of lime

½ teaspoon salt

6 small (6" to 7") corn tortillas

Chopped fresh cilantro

Queso fresco (optional)

Heat the oil in a large skillet over medium-high heat. Set aside 3 tablespoons of the onion. Add the remaining onion and the mushrooms to the skillet. Cook, stirring frequently, for 10 minutes, or until the onion is tender and the mushrooms begin to brown.

Add the garlic, cumin, oregano, and chili powder. Cook, stirring frequently, for 30 seconds, or until the garlic is fragrant. Add the orange juice, lime juice, and salt. Cook for 2 to 3 minutes, or until the juice reduces.

Warm the tortillas in the microwave or a skillet according to package directions.

Spoon the mushroom mixture into the tortillas and garnish with the reserved raw onion, the cilantro, and queso fresco (if using). Squeeze lime juice on top, using the reserved lime wedges.

NUTRITION PER SERVING: 498 calories, 61 g carbs, 8 g fiber, 11 g protein, 25 g total fat, 3 g saturated fat, 616 mg sodium

warm butternut squash and kale salad

Recipe by Lydia Maruniak

makes 2 servings

total time: 30 minutes

If you tend to suffer from "pumpkin fatigue" every fall (and who doesn't, after all those pumpkin lattes, beers, and pies), give butternut squash a try. One cup of the slightly sweet gourd supplies more than 400 percent of your daily need for vitamin A in the form of beta-carotene. This hearty salad—topped with walnuts and goat cheese—is a meal unto itself. But extra-hungry runners can make it even more substantial by tossing in a can of drained white cannellini beans or some cooked orzo.

- 1 small (about 1 pound) butternut squash, peeled and cut into ½" chunks
- 3 tablespoons extra-virgin olive oil
- ½ teaspoon salt, plus more to taste
- Ground black pepper
- ¼ cup chopped walnuts
- 2 teaspoons apple cider vinegar
- ½ teaspoon Dijon mustard
- ¼ teaspoon cayenne pepper
- 1 clove garlic, minced
- 2 large bunches kale
- ⅛ red onion, chopped
- 2 tablespoons crumbled goat cheese (try honey-infused goat cheese for some sweetness)

Preheat the oven to 450°F. Toss the squash in a bowl with 1 tablespoon of the oil. Spread on a foil-lined baking sheet. Lightly season to taste with salt and pepper. Bake for 15 to 20 minutes, or until tender and starting to brown.

Meanwhile, spread the walnuts on a small baking sheet and put it in the same oven. Toast for 2 minutes and remove from the oven.

In a small bowl, combine the vinegar, mustard, cayenne, ½ teaspoon salt, and a generous amount of black pepper. While whisking, drizzle in the remaining 2 tablespoons oil. Stir in the garlic.

Remove the stems from the kale, and chop or tear the leaves into 1" to 2" pieces. Rinse the kale in a colander.

Into a large skillet over medium-high heat, gradually add the wet kale and cook, stirring constantly, for 5 minutes, or until the kale is bright green and slightly wilted. Remove from the heat. Transfer to a large bowl and toss with the dressing, onion, walnuts, and a pinch of salt.

Pile the dressed greens in the center of 2 plates. Top with the cooked squash and goat cheese.

NUTRITION PER SERVING: 441 calories, 30 g carbs, 6 g fiber, 10 g protein, 35 g total fat, 6.5 g saturated fat, 812 mg sodium

grilled asparagus

Recipe by Yishane Lee

makes 4 servings

total time: 15 minutes

A cup of cooked asparagus contains just 40 calories but packs a big nutritional punch. It provides 115 percent of your daily need for vitamin K and 68 percent of your DV for folate, a B vitamin important for new cell growth. If you're not cooking the asparagus right after purchasing, wrap the bunches in a damp paper towel or place upright in an inch of water and cover until you're ready to use.

1 tablespoon balsamic vinegar

1 tablespoon extra-virgin olive oil

1 clove garlic, minced

Salt and ground black pepper

1 bunch (about 1 pound) asparagus spears, tough ends removed

Preheat a grill. In a small bowl, combine the vinegar, oil, garlic, and salt and pepper to taste.

Brush the asparagus with the mixture. Place the spears directly on the grill or on a piece of foil over the grill. Cook, turning the spears over as they begin to brown, for 5 minutes for thin spears and 8 minutes for thick ones, or until tender.

NUTRITION PER SERVING: 57 calories, 5 g carbs, 2 g fiber, 3 g protein, 4 g total fat, 0.5 g saturated fat, 149 mg sodium

steamed and sautéed sugar snap peas

Recipe by Pam Anderson

makes 4 servings

total time: 15 minutes

A cross between snow peas and English peas, sugar snap peas provide 2 grams of fiber, 63 percent of your daily need for vitamin C, and just 26 calories in 1 cup. Their subtly sweet flavor comes through when they are eaten raw or barely cooked, as in this steam-and-sauté preparation from Runner's World *contributing chef Pam Anderson.*

- 1 pound sugar snap peas, stems and tough strings removed
- ¼ cup water
- 1 tablespoon extra-virgin olive oil
- Salt
- 2 tablespoons chopped fresh mint, or any fresh herb
- 1½ teaspoons lemon zest

In a large skillet, combine the snap peas, water, oil, and a pinch of salt. Heat on high and let the peas steam for 3 minutes, or until bright green and crisp-tender.

Once the water evaporates, continue to cook the peas, stirring frequently, for 2 minutes. Turn off the heat and stir in the mint and lemon zest.

NUTRITION PER SERVING: 85 calories, 10 g carbs, 3 g fiber, 3 g protein, 4 g total fat, 0.5 g saturated fat, 53 mg sodium

maple-glazed brussels sprouts

Recipe by Matthew Kadey, MS, RD

makes 4 servings

total time: 25 minutes

Brussels sprouts, like their larger cousin the cabbage, contain sulforaphane, a compound that inhibits the DNA damage that is linked to cancer. Packed with vitamins C and K, Brussels sprouts can also help lower levels of harmful LDL (or so-called "bad cholesterol"). Frozen sprouts are a quick and convenient option for this recipe—just be sure to thoroughly defrost and dry them before using. When buying fresh sprouts, look for a bright green color and firm, tight heads. Although they're harder to find, Brussels sprouts still on the stalk will stay fresher longer.

16 ounces fresh or frozen Brussels sprouts

2 tablespoons maple syrup

1 tablespoon extra-virgin olive oil

2 teaspoons grainy mustard

Salt

Preheat the oven to 400°F. Trim the bottoms off the Brussels sprouts and slice them in half. (If using frozen Brussels sprouts, defrost them and pat them dry with paper towels first.)

In a large bowl, whisk together the maple syrup, oil, mustard, and salt to taste. Add the sprouts and toss to coat with the maple mixture. Transfer to a roasting pan and cook for 20 minutes, stirring once, until the sprouts begin to soften and brown.

NUTRITION PER SERVING: 108 calories, 17 g carbs, 4 g fiber, 4 g protein, 4 g total fat, 0.5 g saturated fat, 177 mg sodium

swiss chard with toasted quinoa and tomato

Recipe by Liz Applegate, PhD

makes 6 servings

total time: 35 minutes

As you'll find with this hearty side dish, toasting quinoa in a saucepan before simmering it in water brings out its nutty flavor. The high-protein whole grain is also a good source of fiber, providing 5 grams per cooked cup. For an even more colorful dish (and an antioxidant boost), use rainbow Swiss chard, which has yellow, orange, pink, and red stalks.

- 2 tablespoons extra-virgin olive oil
- 1 cup quinoa, rinsed
- 3 cups water
- ½ red onion, chopped
- 3 cloves garlic, minced
- 6 cups Swiss chard leaves (about ½ pound), chiffonade (thin strips made by laying the leaves together, rolling like a cigar, and slicing crosswise)
- 1 large tomato, diced
- ½ teaspoon red-pepper flakes
- ⅓ cup freshly grated Parmesan cheese
- Salt and ground black pepper

Heat 1 tablespoon of the oil in a medium saucepan over medium-high heat. Add the quinoa and toast, stirring occasionally, for 4 minutes. Add the water, reduce the heat to low, and simmer for 15 minutes, or until the quinoa is tender. Drain off any remaining water.

Meanwhile, add the remaining 1 tablespoon oil to a large skillet over medium heat. Add the onion and garlic and cook, stirring frequently, for 5 minutes, or until the onion softens.

Add the Swiss chard and cook, stirring frequently, for 4 minutes, or until wilted. Add the tomato and cook until heated through.

Fold in the quinoa, stirring well to combine. Add the pepper flakes and cheese. Season to taste with salt and pepper. Stir again. Let stand for 3 to 5 minutes to blend the flavors.

NUTRITION PER SERVING: 182 calories, 22 g carbs, 3 g fiber, 7 g protein, 8 g total fat, 1.5 g saturated fat, 153 mg sodium

garlicky greens

Recipe by Scott Jurek

makes 4 servings

total time: 15 minutes

Scott Jurek grew up on what he calls a "typical meat-and-potatoes diet." But the ultrarunner (who won the Western States 100-Mile Endurance Run seven times) has been a vegan—eating no animal products—since 1999. "I was in physical therapy school and saw all this chronic illness," he says. "I decided to make a change." Naturally, vegetables of all kinds, including dark leafy greens, make up much of his diet. He likes to prepare this recipe with black kale—also called Tuscan kale, dinosaur kale, or Lacinato kale—but any type of cooking greens will work.

---

1 tablespoon extra-virgin olive oil

2 cloves garlic, minced

1 jalapeño chile pepper, seeded and minced (optional), wear plastic gloves when handling

1 bunch kale, collards, or chard (tough stems removed), coarsely chopped

½ teaspoon salt or tamari

Heat the oil in a large skillet over medium heat. Add the garlic and chile pepper (if using) and cook, stirring constantly, for 1 to 2 minutes until the garlic is golden and fragrant. Add the greens and salt or tamari. Cook, stirring frequently, for 5 to 8 minutes, or until the greens are wilted and tender.

NUTRITION PER SERVING: 50 calories, 4 g carbs, 1 g fiber, 1 g protein, 4 g total fat, 0.5 g saturated fat, 305 mg sodium

roasted sweet potato wedges

Recipe by Scott Jurek

makes 4 servings

total time: 35 minutes

"I usually make potatoes at least once a week," says ultrarunner Scott Jurek. "I look for different types—purple potatoes, Yukon Golds, sweet potatoes." Despite their reputation as being nutrient poor, potatoes are actually an excellent source of carbohydrates, fiber (as long as you eat the skin), potassium, and vitamin C. Slicing them into wedges shortens the cooking time, while roasting brings out their natural sweetness.

4 sweet potatoes, sliced into wedges

1 tablespoon extra-virgin olive oil

1 teaspoon salt

1 teaspoon paprika

1 teaspoon crushed dried rosemary

Preheat the oven to 375°F. In a large bowl, toss the sweet potatoes with the oil, salt, paprika, and rosemary. Arrange on a lightly greased baking sheet. Bake for 20 to 30 minutes, or until the potatoes are cooked through and lightly browned.

NUTRITION PER SERVING: 132 calories, 23 g carbs, 4 g fiber, 2 g protein, 4 g total fat, 0.5 g saturated fat, 652 mg sodium

mashed rutabagas

Recipe by Matthew Kadey, MS, RD

makes 4 servings

total time: 25 minutes

Mashed rutabagas provide a welcome alternative to bland mashed potatoes. This large root vegetable, with a purple skin that fades to cream, has a sweet flavor and slightly peppery bite. A cup of cubed rutabaga contains more than half the daily requirement for vitamin C and 4 grams of heart-healthy fiber.

2 pounds rutabagas, peeled and cubed

2 tablespoons butter

⅓ cup low-fat milk

2 tablespoons chopped fresh sage

1 tablespoon grainy or Dijon mustard

Salt and ground black pepper

Boil a large pot of water over high heat. Add the rutabagas and cook for 20 minutes, or until they're easily pierced with a fork. Turn off the heat, drain the rutabagas, and return them to the pot.

Using a potato masher, lightly mash the rutabagas. Add the butter, milk, sage, and mustard. Season to taste with salt and pepper. Continue mashing until nearly smooth.

NUTRITION PER SERVING: 137 calories, 17 g carbs, 5 g fiber, 3 g protein, 7 g total fat, 4 g saturated fat, 320 mg sodium

butternut squash with pecans and cranberries

Recipe by Yishane Lee

makes 4 servings

total time: 50 minutes

This delicious, healthy side dish is impressive enough to serve at the holidays but easy enough to make anytime. It provides an irresistible mix of flavors and textures, thanks to the crunchy pecans and sweet cranberries. Butternut squash is a rich source of carbohydrates and an ideal choice the night before a long run.

- ½ cup chopped pecans
- 1 tablespoon extra-virgin olive oil
- 1 large onion, finely chopped
- 2 to 3 cloves garlic, finely chopped
- 2¼ pounds butternut squash, peeled, seeded, and cut into ½" cubes
- Pinch of cayenne pepper
- Salt and ground black pepper
- ½ cup dried cranberries
- 3 tablespoons chopped fresh parsley
- ¼ cup grated Parmesan cheese (optional; omit for a vegan dish)

Heat a large skillet over medium heat. Add the pecans and toast, stirring often to avoid burning, for 6 minutes. Remove them from the skillet.

Heat the same skillet over medium-low heat. Add the oil, onion, and garlic. Cook, stirring occasionally, for 5 minutes, or until the onion begins to soften.

Add the squash, cover, and cook, stirring occasionally, for 20 to 30 minutes, or until tender but still holding its shape.

Add the cayenne and season to taste with salt and black pepper. Stir in half of the pecans, cranberries, parsley, and cheese, if using. Transfer to a serving bowl. Garnish with remaining pecans, cranberries, parsley, and cheese, if using.

NUTRITION PER SERVING: 301 calories, 48 g carbs, 8 g fiber, 4 g protein, 14 g total fat, 1.5 g saturated fat, 159 mg sodium

hearty red scalloped potatoes

Recipe by Liz Applegate, PhD

makes 4 to 6 servings

total time: 55 minutes

Scalloped potatoes are traditionally made with plenty of heavy cream and cheese, which add rich flavor—and a huge amount of unhealthy saturated fat. But you can save calories and slash the fat by swapping out the cream for fat-free milk and by using less cheese. The result is still a richly satisfying side dish, but one that will fuel your running rather than weigh you down.

- **6 red potatoes, cut into ½" slices**
- **3 tablespoons whole wheat flour**
- **1½ ounces Gruyere cheese, shredded**
- **1½ ounces Parmesan cheese, grated**
- **½ teaspoon garlic salt**
- **1 shallot, finely chopped**
- **Ground black pepper**
- **1 cup fat-free milk, warmed**

Preheat the oven to 400°F. Coat the bottom of a 2-quart rectangular baking dish with cooking spray.

Line the baking dish with one-third of the potatoes. Sprinkle with 1 tablespoon of the flour, one-third of the Gruyere, one-third of the Parmesan, one-third of the garlic salt, one-third of the shallot, and a sprinkle of black pepper. Repeat the layers two more times.

Pour the milk over the top. Cover with foil and bake for 25 minutes. Uncover and bake 20 minutes longer, or until the potatoes are tender and the cheese is browned. Let sit for 10 minutes before serving.

NUTRITION PER SERVING: 367 calories, 62 g carbs, 6 g fiber, 17 g protein, 7 g total fat, 4 g saturated fat, 363 mg sodium

Desserts

roasted pink grapefruit with honey yogurt

Recipe by Gesine Bullock-Prado

makes 2 servings

total time: 15 minutes

When Runner's World *contributing pastry chef Gesine Bullock-Prado needs a break from carb-packed baked goods, she likes to roast grapefruit with a touch of sugar to bring out the tart fruit's natural sweetness. While all grapefruit is an excellent source of vitamin C (one fruit provides more than 100 percent of your daily need), pink varieties also contain more than half your daily requirement for vitamin A, as well as lycopene. This antioxidant gives the fruit its color and is linked to lower incidences of some cancers. For the ideal recovery snack, enjoy the whole dessert yourself, rather than dividing into two servings.*

1 cup low-fat plain Greek yogurt

2 teaspoons honey

1 pink grapefruit, peeled, sectioned, and white membranes removed

2 teaspoons sugar

In a small mixing bowl, stir together the yogurt and honey. Divide between 2 small serving bowls.

Preheat the broiler on high and place a rack about 4" from the heat. Line a baking tray with parchment paper.

Spread the fruit out on the baking tray. Sprinkle with the sugar and broil for 3 minutes, or until caramelized. Divide the grapefruit between the serving bowls, fanning the fruit out on top of the yogurt, and serve.

NUTRITION PER SERVING: 139 calories, 23 g carbs, 1 g fiber, 9 g protein, 2 g total fat, 2 g saturated fat, 33 mg sodium

marinated peaches

Recipe by Pam Anderson

makes 6 servings

total time: 2 hours 10 minutes (including marinating time)

Fresh, sweet, juicy peaches are a summer treat, delicious and perfect in their own right. But marinating peaches in wine or sparkling cider adds an extra dimension of flavor that elevates the fruit a step higher. Choose peaches that are firm to the touch—ones that are overly soft or have bruises will be mushy. Different varieties have varying amounts of red coloring in their skin, so don't assume a red blush indicates ripeness. Let very firm peaches ripen at room temperature for a few days. They're ready to eat when they smell sweet and give slightly when touched.

---

6 fresh peaches, peeled, pitted, and sliced

1½ cups fruity white wine, such as Chardonnay, Moscato, or Riesling, or sparkling cider

¾ cup sugar

½ teaspoon ground cinnamon

In a bowl, combine the peaches, wine or cider, sugar, and cinnamon. Let the mixture stand at room temperature for 30 minutes, or cover and refrigerate for up to 2 hours. When ready to eat, spoon the fruit and their juices into bowls and serve as is or with a scoop of vanilla ice cream.

NUTRITION PER SERVING (WITH WINE): 206 calories, 43 g carbs, 2 g fiber, 1 g protein, 1 g total fat, 0 g saturated fat, 168 mg sodium

NUTRITION PER SERVING (WITH SPARKLING CIDER): 168 calories, 43 g carbs, 2 g fiber, 1 g protein, 1 g total fat, 0 g saturated fat, 0 mg sodium

strawberry shortcake with whipped ricotta

Recipe by the Rodale Test Kitchen

makes 6 servings

total time: 35 minutes

This classic summer dessert gets a healthy upgrade by swapping out the whipped cream for protein-rich ricotta cheese. Strawberries get their bright red color from antioxidant compounds called anthocyanins, which are also found in other red and blue fruits and can help reduce inflammation. Warmth and moisture are strawberries' worst enemies, so store the fruit in the refrigerator until an hour before using, then rinse and pat dry.

SHORTCAKE

- 1½ cups all-purpose flour
- 2 teaspoons baking powder
- ½ teaspoon baking soda
- 1 tablespoon granulated sugar
- ½ teaspoon salt
- 3 tablespoons butter
- ¾ cup buttermilk
- 2 pints strawberries, hulled and sliced (2 to 3 cups)

TOPPING

- 1 cup part-skim ricotta cheese
- ¼ cup confectioner's sugar
- 1 teaspoon vanilla extract

Preheat the oven to 375°F. Lightly coat a baking sheet with cooking spray.

TO MAKE THE SHORTCAKE: In a mixing bowl, combine the flour, baking powder, baking soda, granulated sugar, and salt. Cut the butter into the dry ingredients with a pastry cutter or 2 butter knives (moving the knives in opposite directions), until crumbly (this creates a flakier shortcake). Add the buttermilk, stirring with a fork until just moistened.

Transfer the dough onto a floured board. Knead a few times, until the dough is smooth in appearance. Pat the dough into an 6" round about ¾" thick. Using a 2½"-round biscuit cutter, cut the dough into rounds, gathering scraps and repatting as necessary. Place on the baking sheet. Bake for 10 to 12 minutes, or until golden brown. Place on a wire rack to cool.

TO MAKE THE TOPPING: In a mixing bowl, combine the ricotta, confectioner's sugar, and vanilla extract. Beat with an electric mixer on medium-high for 1 minute, or until smooth.

When the biscuits are cool, split them in half. Top one biscuit half with about ¼ cup strawberries and ¼ cup whipped ricotta, followed by the other biscuit half. Top again with strawberries and finish with a big dollop of the whipped ricotta.

NUTRITION PER SERVING: 300 calories, 43 g carbs, 3 g fiber, 10 g protein, 10 g total fat, 6 g saturated fat, 618 mg sodium

apple crumble

Recipe by Matt Goulding

makes 4 servings

total time: 40 minutes

These individual dishes of sweet-tart roasted apples are a deeply satisfying end to a meal. What makes this so special is the topping: The oats and almonds give this dish a shot of fiber, healthy fat, and antioxidants, while the crunchy texture offers a rewarding contrast to the soft, cooked apples. If you don't have ramekins, you can bake the dessert in a small 1-quart dish.

- **2 Granny Smith apples, peeled, cored, and cut into wedges**
- **½ cup apple juice**
- **4 tablespoons packed brown sugar**
- **¼ teaspoon ground cinnamon**
- **¼ teaspoon ground nutmeg**
- **1 cup old-fashioned rolled oats**
- **Pinch of salt**
- **2 tablespoons chilled butter, cut into small pieces**
- **¼ cup chopped almonds**
- **Whipped cream**

Preheat the oven to 400°F. In a large mixing bowl, combine the apples, apple juice, 2 tablespoons of the brown sugar, ⅛ teaspoon of the cinnamon, and ⅛ teaspoon of the nutmeg.

In a separate bowl, combine the oats and salt with the remaining 2 tablespoons brown sugar, ⅛ teaspoon cinnamon, and ⅛ teaspoon nutmeg. Add the butter and work the mixture with your fingertips until it comes together in moist clumps. Add the almonds and work them in.

Divide the apple mixture among four 1-cup ramekins or a 1-quart round or square baking dish. Top with the oat mixture. Bake for 25 minutes, or until the apples are hot and bubbling and the crumble has begun to brown. Let cool for a few minutes. Serve with a dollop of whipped cream.

NUTRITION PER SERVING: 307 calories, 43 g carbohydrates, 5 g fiber, 6 g protein, 14 g total fat, 5 g saturated fat, 120 mg sodium

chocolate-berry crisp

Recipe by Liz Applegate, PhD

makes 8 servings

total time: 50 minutes

Crunchy oats, sweet berries, and rich, melted dark chocolate make this a truly satisfying—yet still healthy—indulgence. The berries provide antioxidants key for recovery and (along with the oats) a dose of fiber.

- 2 bags (12 ounces each) frozen mixed berries, such as strawberries, blackberries, raspberries, and blueberries, thawed and drained, or 5 cups fresh berries
- 2 to 3 tablespoons cornstarch
- 2 tablespoons honey
- 1 cup old-fashioned rolled oats
- ⅓ cup toasted wheat germ
- ½ cup packed brown sugar
- 1 teaspoon ground cinnamon
- 1 cup chopped almonds
- ⅓ cup dark or bittersweet chocolate chips
- Vanilla ice cream

Preheat the oven to 350°F. In a bowl, mix the berries and cornstarch. (If using thawed frozen fruit, use the greater amount of cornstarch.) Pour the fruit into an 8" x 8" glass baking dish.

In a small bowl, combine the honey, oats, wheat germ, brown sugar, cinnamon, and almonds. Spread over the berry mixture. Bake for 30 minutes.

Remove the dish from the oven and top evenly with the chocolate chips. Return the dish to the oven and bake for 10 minutes, or until the chocolate is melted. Serve warm topped with a small scoop of vanilla ice cream.

NUTRITION PER SERVING: 296 calories, 41 g carbs, 7 g fiber, 8 g protein, 13 g total fat, 2 g saturated fat, 5 mg sodium

cranberry and walnut dark chocolate bark

Recipe by Ashley Gartland and the Rodale Test Kitchen

makes about 15 pieces

total time: 1 hour 45 minutes (includes cooling time)

There's good reason for runners to indulge in chocolate—dark chocolate, that is. Research shows that eating moderate amounts of dark chocolate can lower rates of stroke, high blood pressure, and heart disease, thanks to its high concentrations of powerful antioxidants called flavonols. Research also shows that people who eat chocolate at least a few times per week weigh less than those who rarely eat it. The key is to stick with chocolate that's at least 60 percent cocoa to get the highest concentration of health-boosting antioxidants—and limit your serving to 1 or 2 ounces, to keep calories and fat in check. This sweet and nutty homemade dark chocolate bark is a great substitute for less healthy store-bought candy bars and provides a good dose of cocoa flavonols.

---

16 ounces dark chocolate (60% cacao or higher), coarsely chopped

½ cup, plus 2 tablespoons coarsely chopped dried cranberries (or try dried tart cherries, dried blueberries, or dried currants)

½ cup, plus 2 tablespoons coarsely chopped walnuts (or try pistachios, almonds, or pecans)

½ teaspoon fine sea salt (optional)

Line a rimmed 15" x 10" baking sheet with waxed paper. Place the chocolate in a glass bowl and set it in the microwave. Melt the chocolate on medium power for 3 to 5 minutes, stirring every 30 seconds at first. Once the pieces start to soften, stir every 15 seconds, being careful not to microwave longer than needed.

Stir the ½ cup cranberries and ½ cup walnuts into the chocolate. Pour the mixture onto the baking sheet. Spread into a ¼" layer. Sprinkle the top of the chocolate with the remaining 2 tablespoons cranberries and 2 tablespoons walnuts. Sprinkle with the sea salt, if using. Let the chocolate cool for 1 to 1½ hours.

Once hard, break the bark into about 15 pieces. Store in a container with a tight-fitting lid.

NUTRITION PER PIECE: 213 calories, 25 g carbs, 1 g fiber, 4 g protein, 13 g total fat, 6 g saturated fat, 63 mg sodium

mocha-cinnamon pudding

Recipe by Pam Anderson

makes 4 servings

total time: 10 minutes

Easy to make and tastier than store-bought, homemade pudding is a dessert you can feel good about. With fewer than 250 calories, it provides protein, calcium, and antioxidants from cinnamon that protect against diabetes and heart disease. A touch of coffee brings out the best in chocolate by subtly rounding out the flavor. Enjoy the pudding as is, or try it topped with Whipped Ricotta (page 238).

¼ cup sugar

3 tablespoons cornstarch

2 teaspoons instant coffee mix or espresso powder

½ teaspoon ground cinnamon

Pinch of salt

2 cups low-fat chocolate milk or chocolate soy milk

2 ounces bittersweet chocolate, very finely chopped (about ⅓ cup)

1 teaspoon vanilla extract

In a large saucepan (without any heat), whisk together the sugar, cornstarch, coffee, cinnamon, and salt.

Turn the heat to medium and whisk in the milk. When the milk begins to bubble, reduce the heat to low and cook, stirring occasionally at first, then frequently and constantly at the end, for 5 minutes, or until the mixture thickens to pudding consistency. Remove the saucepan from the heat.

Add the chocolate and vanilla extract, whisking until the chocolate is smooth. Serve warm. Or pour into 4 small ramekins or dessert bowls, and place plastic wrap directly on the pudding surface to keep a skin from forming. Refrigerate for up to 5 days.

NUTRITION PER SERVING: 237 calories, 37 g carbs, 3 g fiber, 6 g protein, 8 g total fat, 5 g saturated fat, 151 mg sodium

chocolate-oatmeal cookies

Recipe by Liz Applegate, PhD

makes 30

total time: 50 minutes

Chocolate chips, walnuts, and oats give these cookies a chewy and crunchy texture. They use less sugar than many traditional chocolate chip cookies, but have plenty of rich sweetness thanks to the combination of brown sugar, dark honey, and cocoa powder.

- 6 **tablespoons butter, at room temperature**
- ½ **cup packed brown sugar**
- ½ **cup granulated sugar**
- 3 **tablespoons dark honey, such as buckwheat**
- 2 **eggs**
- 1 **teaspoon vanilla extract**
- ½ **cup all-purpose flour**
- ½ **cup whole wheat flour**
- 1 **teaspoon baking soda**
  Pinch of salt
- ¼ **cup unsweetened cocoa powder**
- 2 **cups quick-cooking oats**
- ¾ **cup dark chocolate chips, or 4 ounces chopped dark chocolate**
- ½ **cup chopped walnuts or pecans**

Preheat the oven to 375°F. Coat a baking sheet with cooking spray or line it with parchment paper.

In the bowl of an electric mixer or in a mixing bowl, combine the butter, brown sugar, granulated sugar, and honey. Beat on high speed until smooth and creamy. Add the eggs and vanilla extract and beat on low speed to blend well.

In another bowl, combine the all-purpose flour, whole wheat flour, baking soda, salt, and cocoa powder. Stir until well combined. Add to the wet mixture. Stir in the oats, chocolate, and nuts.

Spoon the batter in 1-tablespoon mounds onto the baking sheet. Bake for 10 to 12 minutes, or until set to the touch.

NUTRITION PER COOKIE: 124 calories, 23 g carbs, 2 g fiber, 3 g protein, 7 g total fat, 3 g saturated fat, 74 mg sodium

frozen peanut butter balls

Recipe by Gregg Avedon

makes 30 balls

**total time: 2 hours 15 minutes
(includes cooling time)**

*Next time you get a chocolate–peanut butter craving, put down the
peanut butter cups and reach for one of these crunchy treats instead—
they're particularly delicious just as they begin to melt. Peanut butter
provides heart-healthy unsaturated fats while banana adds a sweet touch.*

- **2 cups crunchy natural
  peanut butter**
- **2 scoops chocolate soy
  protein powder (about
  ¼ cup)**
- **2 extra-ripe bananas,
  mashed**
- **2 tablespoons ground
  flaxseeds**

Line the bottom of a large plastic storage container with parchment paper. In a bowl, combine the peanut butter, protein powder, bananas, and flaxseeds. Stir until thoroughly mixed.

Using your hands, roll the mixture into 30 walnut-size balls.
Place the balls in the container with parchment paper in between
each layer. Refrigerate or freeze for at least 2 hours before
serving.

NUTRITION PER TWO PEANUT BUTTER BALLS: 239 calories, 13 g carbs, 3 g fiber,
12 g protein, 18 g total fat, 3 g saturated fat, 173 mg sodium

super fudgy brownies

Recipe by Liz Applegate, PhD

makes 12 brownies

**total time: 35 minutes
(plus cooling time)**

*These moist, chewy brownies have plenty of rich chocolatey flavor—
with a fraction of the fat and calories found in many traditional recipes.
Wheat germ and oats add fiber and vitamins, while the milk powder
provides a calcium boost.*

- **6 ounces semisweet chocolate chips (about 1 cup)**
- **3 tablespoons butter**
- **¾ cup quick-cooking oats**
- **⅓ cup toasted wheat germ**
- **⅓ cup fat-free dry milk powder**
- **½ cup chopped walnuts**
- **1 egg**
- **2 egg whites**
- **½ cup packed brown sugar**
- **1 teaspoon vanilla extract**

Preheat the oven to 350°F. Coat an 8" x 8" baking dish with cooking spray.

Put the chocolate and butter in a microwaveable dish. Melt in the microwave on medium power for 30 to 45 seconds.

In a bowl, stir together the oats, wheat germ, milk powder, and walnuts.

In the bowl of an electric mixer, beat together the egg and egg whites, brown sugar, and vanilla extract. Stir in the melted chocolate and beat until smooth. Stir in the oat mixture. Pour the batter into the baking dish. Bake for 20 to 25 minutes, or until a toothpick inserted in the middle comes out clean.

When the brownies are cool, cut them with a sharp knife coated with cooking spray.

NUTRITION PER BROWNIE: 197 calories, 22 g carbs, 2 g fiber, 5 g protein, 11 g total fat, 5 g saturated fat, 29 mg sodium

long-run cake with peanut butter–cream cheese frosting

Recipe by Gesine Bullock-Prado

makes 12 cakes

total time: 40 minutes

These gluten-free, mini cake loaves, created by Runner's World *contributing pastry chef Gesine Bullock-Prado, contain no added oils or butter, yet stay incredibly moist thanks to applesauce and black beans (the latter of which also lends dense, fudgy texture). Without the frosting, the cake is ideal fuel before a long run. Or, save them until after you run and spread them with the rich peanut butter–cream cheese frosting for a well-deserved treat.*

CAKE

- 1 cup unsweetened applesauce
- 1 can (15.5 ounces) black beans, rinsed and drained
- 1½ cups oat flour
- 1 cup high-quality unsweetened cocoa powder
- 2 teaspoons baking powder
- 1 teaspoon salt
- 1 cup agave syrup
- 2 eggs
- ¼ cup brewed coffee
- 1 teaspoon vanilla extract

FROSTING (OPTIONAL)

- 2 packages (8 ounces each) cream cheese
- ¼ cup agave syrup
- ¼ cup natural smooth peanut butter
- Pinch of salt

Preheat the oven to 350°F. Coat 12 mini (2¼" x 4") loaf pans with cooking spray.

TO MAKE THE CAKE: In a food processor, combine the applesauce and beans. Process until smooth.

In a medium bowl, whisk together the oat flour, cocoa, baking powder, and salt.

In the bowl of an electric mixer fitted with the whisk attachment, whisk together the agave and eggs until light and foamy. Reduce the mixer speed to medium-low and pour in the coffee. Mix until combined. Add the bean mixture and vanilla extract. Beat until combined. Add the oat-cocoa mixture all at once. Beat on low until just moist, then increase the speed and beat for 30 seconds, or until smooth.

Pour the batter into the mini loaf pans (the batter should reach two-thirds of the way up the loaf pan). Bake for 20 to 25 minutes, or until a cake springs back when poked.

TO MAKE THE FROSTING (IF USING): In the bowl of an electric mixer fitted with the paddle attachment, combine the cream cheese, agave, peanut butter, and salt. Beat until smooth. If the mixture is too soupy, refrigerate for 1 hour, or until firm. When the loaves are cool, remove them from the pans and top them with the frosting, spreading with a small offset spatula or the back of a small teaspoon.

NUTRITION PER CAKE (NO FROSTING): 186 calories, 38 g carbs, 4 g fiber, 4 g protein, 2 g total fat, 0 g saturated fat, 377 mg sodium

NUTRITION PER CAKE (WITH FROSTING): 365 calories, 46 g carbs, 4 g fiber, 8 g protein, 18 g total fat, 8 g saturated fat, 537 mg sodium

sticky toffee figgy cupcakes

Recipe by Gesine Bullock-Prado

makes 16 cupcakes

total time: 1 hour

It's hard to believe that these dense, moist, indulgent-tasting cupcakes—topped with a sweet caramel sauce—have only 125 calories each. The secret is soaking the dried figs in coffee, which keeps the batter moist while adding lots of rich, figgy flavor. Try one for a carb-packed prerun snack.

CAKE

- 1½ cups finely chopped dried figs
- 1 cup hot coffee
- 1 teaspoon baking soda
- 2 large eggs, at room temperature
- ½ cup packed brown sugar
- 2 tablespoons honey
- ½ cup canned pumpkin puree (not pumpkin pie filling)
- 1 cup whole wheat pastry flour
- ½ teaspoon salt
- 1 teaspoon baking powder
- ½ teaspoon ground cinnamon
- ¼ teaspoon ground nutmeg

SAUCE

- 1 tablespoon butter
- 1 tablespoon almond oil or canola oil
- 1 tablespoon honey
- 2 tablespoons packed brown sugar
- Pinch of salt
- ¼ cup fat-free evaporated milk

Preheat the oven to 350°F. Place paper liners in a 12-cup muffin tin.

TO MAKE THE CAKE: Place the figs in a large bowl. Pour the hot coffee over the figs to cover completely. Stir in the baking soda. Allow to sit, undisturbed, for 5 minutes.

In the bowl of an electric mixer fitted with the whisk attachment, combine the eggs, brown sugar, and honey. Whisk for 3 minutes, or until the mixture thickens. Add the pumpkin puree. Mix until just combined.

In a large bowl, stir together the flour, salt, baking powder, cinnamon, and nutmeg.

With the electric mixer running on low speed, add the fig mixture to the egg mixture. Slowly add the flour mixture. Mix until just combined.

Pour the batter into the muffin cups, filling each about three-quarters full. Bake for 20 minutes, or until a cake springs back when gently poked. Pop the cupcakes out and line again with 4 more paper liners. Fill with the remaining batter and bake.

TO MAKE THE SAUCE: In a heavy saucepan, combine the butter, oil, honey, brown sugar, and salt. Stir over medium heat until the sugar has completely melted. While continuously stirring, slowly add the evaporated milk and cook, stirring, for 5 minutes, or until the sauce thickens.

While the cupcakes are still warm, use a toothpick or wooden skewer to poke a few holes in each. Spoon 1 teaspoon of the caramel sauce over each of the cupcakes. Serve immediately, or store them in the refrigerator for a day or two.

NUTRITION PER SERVING: 125 calories, 25 g carbs, 2 g fiber, 2 g protein, 2 g total fat, 1 g saturated fat, 227 mg sodium

soft ginger cookies

Recipe by Gesine Bullock-Prado

makes 30 cookies

total time: 1 hour

Dates are the secret ingredient in these whole grain cookies, keeping them moist and eliminating the need for butter or oil, while also providing fiber and potassium. "The crystallized ginger gives this lovely nugget the perfect bite—spicy and chewy at the same time," says Runner's World *contributing pastry chef Gesine Bullock-Prado.*

- ¾ **cup hot coffee**
- 1 **cup chopped, pitted dried dates**
- ½ **teaspoon baking soda**
- 2 **eggs, at room temperature**
- ¼ **cup blackstrap molasses**
- 1½ **cups spelt flour or whole wheat flour**
- ½ **teaspoon salt**
- 1 **tablespoon ground ginger**
- ½ **teaspoon ground cinnamon**
- ½ **teaspoon ground white pepper**
- ¼ **teaspoon ground cloves**
- ¼ **teaspoon ground nutmeg**
- ½ **cup chopped crystallized ginger**
- ¼ **cup turbinado sugar or granulated sugar**

Preheat the oven to 350°F. Line a baking sheet with parchment paper.

In a small bowl, combine the coffee, dates, and baking soda. Stir, then let the mixture sit for 10 minutes. Transfer the mixture to a food processor and puree until nearly smooth.

In the bowl of an electric mixer fitted with a whisk attachment or in a large mixing bowl, combine the eggs and molasses and whisk together. Continue whisking and add the date puree.

In a small bowl, whisk together the flour, salt, ginger, cinnamon, white pepper, cloves, and nutmeg. Stir into the date mixture until combined. Stir in the ginger pieces until just combined. Freeze the batter for 30 minutes, or until very firm but scoopable.

Using a teaspoon, drop the dough into little mounds, a few inches apart, on the baking sheet. Sprinkle the turbinado or granulated sugar over the cookies. Bake for 10 minutes, or until they feel spongy yet firm and spring back when gently poked. Remove from the baking sheet.

NUTRITION PER COOKIE: 66 calories, 14 g carbs, 1 g fiber, 1 g protein, 1 g total fat, 0 g saturated fat, 68 mg sodium

pumpkin-pecan pie

Recipe by Liz Applegate, PhD

makes 8 servings

total time: 1 hour

Pumpkin pie and pecan pie are two classic holiday desserts. But while the former is a relatively healthy treat that's high in beta-carotene, the latter is loaded with fat and can often pack more than 500 calories per slice. The perfect solution? Merge the two into one delicious pie that provides the crunchy sweetness of candied pecans and the smooth creaminess of pureed pumpkin.

- 1 (9") piecrust, unbaked
- 2 whole eggs
- 1 cup evaporated fat-free milk
- 1 can (15 ounces) pumpkin puree (not pumpkin pie filling)
- 1½ teaspoons ground cinnamon
- ¼ teaspoon ground nutmeg
- ¼ teaspoon ground cloves
- ½ cup, plus ⅓ cup packed brown sugar
- 1 cup pecan halves
- 3 tablespoons butter, melted
- 2 egg whites
- 1 teaspoon vanilla extract

Preheat the oven to 350°F. Place the piecrust in a 9" pie pan.

In the bowl of an electric mixer or in a large mixing bowl, combine the whole eggs, evaporated milk, pumpkin puree, cinnamon, nutmeg, cloves, and the ½ cup brown sugar. Whisk together and pour into the piecrust. Bake for 30 minutes.

Meanwhile, in a medium bowl, combine the pecans and butter, tossing to coat thoroughly. In another bowl, whisk together the egg whites, vanilla extract, and the remaining ⅓ cup brown sugar. Add to the pecans and stir to combine.

After 30 minutes, remove the pie from the oven and spread the pecan mixture on top. Bake for 20 to 25 minutes, or until just set.

NUTRITION PER SERVING: 339 calories, 37 g carbs, 3 g fiber, 8 g protein, 19 g total fat, 6 g saturated fat, 174 mg sodium

THE RUNNER'S PANTRY

Keep your kitchen stocked with these long-lasting staples and you'll have almost everything you need to throw together a healthy, runner-friendly meal in no time.

Canned Beans and Dried Lentils
- Chickpeas
- White beans (such as cannellini and great Northern)
- Dark and light kidney beans
- Pinto beans
- Black beans
- Red, brown, and green dried lentils

Grains
- Brown rice
- Bulgur
- Barley
- Quinoa
- Oats (old-fashioned and steel cut)
- Whole wheat pastry flour

Pasta and Noodles
- Whole wheat pasta (short and long shapes)
- White (semolina) pasta
- Soba noodles

Long-Lasting Produce
- Potatoes (sweet, baking, Yukon Gold, or red-skinned)
- Onions
- Garlic
- Carrots
- Celery
- Canned tomatoes (whole and diced)
- Frozen fruits and vegetables (all kinds)

Canned Fish
- Wild salmon
- Tuna
- Sardines
- Anchovies
- Crab

Dried Fruits
- Dried tart cherries
- Raisins
- Dried blueberries
- Dried apricots

Nuts and Seeds
- Walnuts
- Almonds
- Pecans
- Nut butters
- Ground flaxseed

Oils and Vinegars
- Extra-virgin olive oil
- Canola oil
- Walnut or flaxseed oil
- Balsamic vinegar
- Rice vinegar or sherry vinegar

Flavorings
- Dried herbs and spices (all kinds)
- Jarred pesto
- Roasted red peppers
- Sun-dried tomatoes
- Bottled stir-fry sauce
- Soy sauce
- Dijon mustard
- Chicken, beef, and vegetable broths

SPECIAL RECIPE LISTS

Looking for a prerun meal? Need a vegetarian recipe? Search the Special Recipe Lists to find exactly what you need, whether it's Prerun, Recovery, Fast, Low-Calorie, Vegetarian, Vegan, or Gluten-Free.

Egg and Bean Burrito with Avocado and Yogurt-Lime Sauce (page 34)

Mushroom and Spinach Crepes (page 35)

Corn Tortilla with Fig Jam and Roasted Turkey (page 37)

Breakfast Pita with Apricots, Olives, and Feta Cheese (page 38)

Cashew Butter and Mango Chutney Sandwich (page 41)

Coconut-Almond Energy Bars (page 44)

Cinnamon and Sugar Popcorn (page 49)

Rosemary-Parmesan Popcorn (page 49)

Spiced Pecans (page 50)

Butternut Squash Hummus (page 54)

Sliced Apple with Goat Cheese and Balsamic Vinegar (page 52)

Good-for-You Black Forest Blizzard (page 56)

Crunchy Coffee-Cocoa Shake (page 57)

Maple–Pumpkin Pie Smoothie (page 57)

Blueberry-Oatmeal Smoothie (page 58)

Melon-Mango Shake (page 58)

Orange-Pomegranate Power Smoothie (page 60)

Immune-Boosting Raspberry-Almond Smoothie (page 60)

Spinach-Kiwi Cooler (page 61)

Cherry-Coconut Recovery Shake (page 61)

Thai Beef Salad with Mint (page 67)

Chicken Salad with Peas, Feta, and Mint (page 68)

Tuna Salad with Parsley Dressing (page 69)

Asian Noodle Salad with Eggs and Peanut Dressing (page 70)

Fresh Market Slaw (page 75)

Watermelon and Feta Salad (page 76)

Cantaloupe and Cucumber Salad (page 77)

Tabbouleh (page 80)

Chickpea, Cherry, and Ginger Salad (page 81)

Greek Lima Bean Salad (page 84)

Honey Dressing (page 85)

Mustard and Cumin Vinaigrette (page 85)

Nutty Olive Oil Dressing (page 86)

Blackberry Dressing (page 86)

Chickpea-Pesto Tomato Soup (page 100)

Curried Coconut-Squash Soup (page 102)

Creamy Potato-Spinach Soup (page 105)

Roast Beef Pita with Cucumber-Yogurt Sauce (page 118)

Chicken-Pesto Sandwich (page 119)

Curried Chicken Salad Sandwich with Cranberries and Pine Nuts (page 120)

Mediterranean Pizza with Smoked Ham (page 125)

Fig and Prosciutto Sandwich (page 126)

Smoked Salmon and Veggie Wrap (page 127)

Salmon Salad Sandwich with Chili Aioli (page 128)

Anchovy and Olive Pizza (page 129)

Bean and Shrimp Quesadilla (page 130)

White Bean–Artichoke Wrap (page 131)

Almond Butter and Pear Sandwich (page 134)

Curry Egg Salad Sandwich (page 135)

Basil-Mint Pesto (page 141)

Kale-Almond Pesto (page 142)

Cilantro-Pumpkin Pesto (page 143)

Tagliatelle with Peas, Chile, and Mint (page 144)

Bow-Ties with Tomato and Arugula (page 147)

Portobello and Asparagus Pasta (page 148)

Penne with Sardines, Prosciutto, and Cherry Tomatoes (page 151)

Shrimp, Artichoke, and Pesto Pasta (page 152)

Soba Noodles with Chicken and Peanut Sauce (page 155)

Rigatoni with Chicken Sausage (page 158)

Barbecue Beef Sloppy Joes (page 167)

Thai Beef and Snow Pea Stir-Fry (page 168)

Chicken-Mango Fajitas (page 180)

Grilled Salmon with Lentil Tabbouleh (page 188)

Mini Salmon Cakes with Salsa (page 190)

Barramundi in Saffron Broth (page 194)

Maple-Glazed Arctic Char (page 196)

Sablefish with Pomegranate Syrup (page 197)

Pacific Halibut with Kiwi Salsa (page 198)

Sweet and Sour Shrimp Stir-Fry (page 199)

Garlic Shrimp with White Beans and Tomatoes (page 200)

Jerk Shrimp with Sweet Potato and Black Beans (page 203)

Crab and Black Bean Tacos (page 204)

Crab-and-Lentil-Stuffed Tomato with Yogurt Sauce (page 205)

Coconut-Lime Mussels (page 206)

Chickpea and Spinach Stir-Fry (page 213)

Steel Cut Oatmeal Risotto with Asparagus (page 217)

Mushroom Tacos al Pastor (page 220)

Warm Butternut Squash and Kale Salad (page 221)

Grilled Asparagus (page 222)

Fast—*continued*

Steamed and Sautéed Sugar Snap Peas (page 223)

Maple-Glazed Brussels Sprouts (page 224)

Garlicky Greens (page 228)

Mashed Rutabagas (page 229)

Roasted Pink Grapefruit with Honey Yogurt (page 236)

Mocha-Cinnamon Pudding (page 245)

Low-Calorie
(400 calories or less)

Hearty Whole Grain Muffins (page 16)

Hummingbird Muffins (page 17)

Fresh Fruit Scones (page 18)

Awesome Granola (page 20)

Creamy Cocoa Oatmeal (page 21)

Savory Steel Cut Oatmeal (page 22)

Spiced Breakfast Quinoa (page 23)

Multigrain Pancakes (page 26)

Cinnamon Peach Topping (page 30)

Sweet or Savory Corncakes (page 31)

Mushroom and Spinach Crepes (page 35)

More-Vegetable-Than-Egg Frittata (page 36)

Corn Tortilla with Fig Jam and Roasted Turkey (page 37)

Coconut-Almond Energy Bars (page 44)

Banana-Oat Energy Bars (page 47)

Pumpkin-Cherry Trail Mix (page 48)

Cinnamon and Sugar Popcorn (page 49)

Rosemary-Parmesan Popcorn (page 49)

Spiced Pecans (page 50)

Roasted Almond Butter (page 51)

Sliced Apple with Goat Cheese and Balsamic Vinegar (page 52)

Butternut Squash Hummus (page 54)

Corn-Melon Salsa (page 55)

Good-for-You Black Forest Blizzard (page 56)

Crunchy Coffee-Cocoa Shake (page 57)

Maple–Pumpkin Pie Smoothie (page 57)

Blueberry-Oatmeal Smoothie (page 58)

Melon-Mango Shake (page 58)

Orange-Pomegranate Power Smoothie (page 60)

Cherry-Coconut Recovery Shake (page 61)

Spinach, Bacon, and Sweet Potato Salad (page 64)

Thai Beef Salad with Mint (page 67)

Chicken Salad with Peas, Feta, and Mint (page 68)

Asian Noodle Salad with Eggs and Peanut Dressing (page 70)

Mint Potato Salad (page 73)

Creamy Coleslaw (page 74)

Fresh Market Slaw (page 75)

Watermelon and Feta Salad (page 76)

Cantaloupe and Cucumber Salad (page 77)

Beets with Avocado and Orange (page 78)

Tabbouleh (page 80)

Greek Lima Bean Salad (page 84)

Honey Dressing (page 85)

Mustard and Cumin Vinaigrette (page 85)

Nutty Olive Oil Dressing (page 86)

Blackberry Dressing (page 86)

Thai Avocado Soup (page 90)

Chilled Zucchini Soup (page 92)

Tomatillo Gazpacho (page 93)

Mango Gazpacho (page 95)

Minestrone with Spring Vegetables (page 96)

Potato-Leek Soup (page 98)

Celeriac and Potato Soup (page 99)

Chickpea-Pesto Tomato Soup (page 100)

Curried Coconut-Squash Soup (page 102)

Red Lentil and Black Bean Stew (page 103)

Slow-Cooked Clam Chowder (page 104)

Creamy Potato-Spinach Soup (page 105)

Chicken-Quinoa Soup (page 106)

Crunchy Cocoa Chili (page 111)

Bean and Vegetable Chili (page 113)

Meat and Grain Burgers (page 116)

Roast Beef Pita with Cucumber-Yogurt Sauce (page 118)

Chicken-Pesto Sandwich (page 119)

Chicken Pitas with Sun-Dried Tomato Spread (page 122)

Fig and Prosciutto Sandwich (page 126)

Smoked Salmon and Veggie Wrap (page 127)

Anchovy and Olive Pizza (page 129)

Caramelized Onion and Fig Pizza (page 133)

Quick-and-Easy Marinara (page 138)

Fire-Roasted Meat Sauce (page 139)

Basil-Mint Pesto (page 141)

Kale-Almond Pesto (page 142)

Cilantro-Pumpkin Pesto (page 143)

Pasta Bean Toss (page 150)

Marinated Beef and Veggie Kebabs (page 165)

Meat Loaf (page 166)

Barbecue Beef Sloppy Joes (page 167)

Pork Tenderloin with Winter Vegetables (page 172)

Super-Easy Barbecue Pulled Pork (page 175)

Southern Unfried Chicken (page 178)

Marinated Grilled Chicken
(page 179)

Chicken-Mango Fajitas (page 180)

Chicken Stir-Fry with Green Beans
and Broccoli (page 183)

Chicken with Asparagus,
Mushrooms, and Rice
(page 184)

Mini Salmon Cakes with Salsa
(page 190)

Salmon Coconut Curry (page 191)

Spicy Fish Tacos with Pineapple
Slaw (page 193)

Maple-Glazed Arctic Char
(page 196)

Barramundi in Saffron Broth
(page 194)

Pacific Halibut with Kiwi Salsa
(page 198)

Sablefish with Pomegranate Syrup
(page 197)

Jerk Shrimp with Sweet Potato and
Black Beans (page 203)

Crab and Black Bean Tacos
(page 204)

Crab-and-Lentil-Stuffed Tomato
with Yogurt Sauce (page 205)

Coconut-Lime Mussels (page 206)

Chickpea and Spinach Stir-Fry
(page 213)

Chickpea Spread for Bruschetta
(page 214)

Dal with Cauliflower, Eggplant,
and Zucchini (page 216)

Steel Cut Oatmeal Risotto with
Asparagus (page 217)

Grilled Vegetable Polenta
Casserole (page 219)

Grilled Asparagus (page 222)

Steamed and Sautéed Sugar Snap
Peas (page 223)

Garlicky Greens (page 228)

Maple-Glazed Brussels Sprouts
(page 224)

Swiss Chard with Toasted Quinoa
and Tomato (page 227)

Roasted Sweet Potato Wedges
(page 229)

Mashed Rutabagas (page 229)

Butternut Squash with Pecans and
Cranberries (page 230)

Hearty Red Scalloped Potatoes
(page 233)

Roasted Pink Grapefruit with
Honey Yogurt (page 236)

Marinated Peaches (page 237)

Strawberry Shortcake with
Whipped Ricotta (page 238)

Apple Crumble (page 241)

Chocolate-Berry Crisp (page 242)

Cranberry and Walnut Dark
Chocolate Bark (page 244)

Mocha-Cinnamon Pudding
(page 245)

Chocolate-Oatmeal Cookies
(page 246)

Super Fudgy Brownies (page 249)

Sticky Toffee Figgy Cupcakes
(page 253)

Soft Ginger Cookies (page 254)

Pumpkin-Pecan Pie (page 255)

Vegetarian

Hearty Whole Grain Muffins
(page 16)

Hummingbird Muffins (page 17)

Fresh Fruit Scones (page 18)

Awesome Granola (page 20)

Creamy Cocoa Oatmeal (page 21)

Savory Steel Cut Oatmeal
(page 22)

Stick-with-You Polenta (page 25)

Spiced Breakfast Quinoa (page 23)

Multigrain Pancakes (page 26)

Cinnamon Peach Topping (page 30)

Sweet or Savory Corncakes
(page 31)

Double Vanilla French Toast
(page 32)

Egg and Bean Burrito with
Avocado and Yogurt-Lime
Sauce (page 34)

Mushroom and Spinach Crepes
(page 35)

More-Vegetable-Than-Egg Frittata
(page 36)

Cashew Butter and Mango
Chutney Sandwich (page 41)

Coconut-Almond Energy Bars
(page 44)

Banana-Oat Energy Bars (page 47)

Pumpkin-Cherry Trail Mix
(page 48)

Cinnamon and Sugar Popcorn
(page 49)

Rosemary-Parmesan Popcorn
(page 49)

Spiced Pecans (page 50)

Roasted Almond Butter (page 51)

Sliced Apple with Goat Cheese
and Balsamic Vinegar (page 52)

Butternut Squash Hummus
(page 54)

Corn-Melon Salsa (page 55)

Good-for-You Black Forest Blizzard
(page 56)

Crunchy Coffee-Cocoa Shake
(page 57)

Maple-Pumpkin Pie Smoothie
(page 57)

Blueberry-Oatmeal Smoothie
(page 58)

Melon-Mango Shake (page 58)

Orange-Pomegranate Power
Smoothie (page 60)

Immune-Boosting Raspberry-
Almond Smoothie (page 60)

Spinach-Kiwi Cooler (page 61)

Cherry-Coconut Recovery Shake
(page 61)

Asian Noodle Salad with Eggs and
Peanut Dressing (page 70)

Mint Potato Salad (page 73)

Creamy Coleslaw (page 74)

Fresh Market Slaw (page 75)

Watermelon and Feta Salad
(page 76)

Cantaloupe and Cucumber Salad
(page 77)

Beets with Avocado and Orange
(page 78)

Tabbouleh (page 80)

Chickpea, Cherry, and Ginger
Salad (page 81)

Vegetarian—continued

Caprese Farro Salad (page 83)

Greek Lima Bean Salad (page 84)

Honey Dressing (page 85)

Mustard and Cumin Vinaigrette (page 85)

Nutty Olive Oil Dressing (page 86)

Blackberry Dressing (page 86)

Thai Avocado Soup (page 90)

Mango Gazpacho (page 95)

Minestrone with Spring Vegetables (page 96)

Celeriac and Potato Soup (page 99)

Chickpea-Pesto Tomato Soup (page 100)

Red Lentil and Black Bean Stew (page 103)

Creamy Potato-Spinach Soup (page 105)

Crunchy Cocoa Chili (page 111)

White Bean–Artichoke Wrap (page 131)

Caramelized Onion and Fig Pizza (page 133)

Almond Butter and Pear Sandwich (page 134)

Curry Egg Salad Sandwich (page 135)

Quick-and-Easy Marinara (page 138)

Basil-Mint Pesto (page 141)

Kale-Almond Pesto (page 142)

Cilantro-Pumpkin Pesto (page 143)

Tagliatelle with Peas, Chile, and Mint (page 144)

Bow-Ties with Tomato and Arugula (page 147)

Portobello and Asparagus Pasta (page 148)

Brown Rice Salad with Curried Tofu (page 210)

Sweet and Sour Tofu Stir-Fry (page 212)

Chickpea and Spinach Stir-Fry (page 213)

Chickpea Spread for Bruschetta (page 214)

Dal with Cauliflower, Eggplant, and Zucchini (page 216)

Steel Cut Oatmeal Risotto with Asparagus (page 217)

Grilled Vegetable Polenta Casserole (page 219)

Mushroom Tacos al Pastor (page 220)

Warm Butternut Squash and Kale Salad (page 221)

Grilled Asparagus (page 222)

Steamed and Sautéed Sugar Snap Peas (page 223)

Maple-Glazed Brussels Sprouts (page 224)

Swiss Chard with Toasted Quinoa and Tomato (page 227)

Garlicky Greens (page 228)

Roasted Sweet Potato Wedges (page 229)

Mashed Rutabagas (page 229)

Butternut Squash with Pecans and Cranberries (page 230)

Hearty Red Scalloped Potatoes (page 233)

Roasted Pink Grapefruit with Honey Yogurt (page 236)

Marinated Peaches (page 237)

Strawberry Shortcake with Whipped Ricotta (page 238)

Apple Crumble (page 241)

Chocolate-Berry Crisp (page 242)

Cranberry and Walnut Dark Chocolate Bark (page 244)

Mocha-Cinnamon Pudding (page 245)

Chocolate-Oatmeal Cookies (page 246)

Super Fudgy Brownies (page 249)

Long-Run Cake with Peanut Butter–Cream Cheese Frosting (page 250)

Sticky Toffee Figgy Cupcakes (page 253)

Soft Ginger Cookies (page 254)

Pumpkin-Pecan Pie (page 255)

Vegan

Spiced Breakfast Quinoa (page 23)

Cinnamon Peach Topping (page 30)

Banana-Oat Energy Bars (page 47)

Pumpkin-Cherry Trail Mix (page 48)

Cinnamon and Sugar Popcorn (page 49)

Spiced Pecans (page 50)

Butternut Squash Hummus (page 54)

Corn-Melon Salsa (page 55)

Maple–Pumpkin Pie Smoothie (page 57)

Spinach-Kiwi Cooler (page 61)

Cherry-Coconut Recovery Shake (page 61)

Mint Potato Salad (page 73)

Beets with Avocado and Orange (page 78)

Mustard and Cumin Vinaigrette (page 85)

Nutty Olive Oil Dressing (page 86)

Minestrone with Spring Vegetables (page 96)

Celeriac and Potato Soup (page 99)

Red Lentil and Black Bean Stew (page 103)

Crunchy Cocoa Chili (page 111)

White Bean–Artichoke Wrap (page 131)

Quick-and-Easy Marinara (page 138)

Brown Rice Salad with Curried Tofu (page 210)

Sweet and Sour Tofu Stir-Fry (page 212)

Chickpea and Spinach Stir-Fry (page 213)

Chickpea Spread for Bruschetta (page 214)

Steel Cut Oatmeal Risotto with Asparagus (page 217)

Mushroom Tacos al Pastor (page 220)

Grilled Asparagus (page 222)

Steamed and Sautéed Sugar Snap
Peas (page 223)

Maple-Glazed Brussels Sprouts
(page 224)

Garlicky Greens (page 228)

Roasted Sweet Potato Wedges
(page 229)

Butternut Squash with Pecans and
Cranberries (page 230)

Marinated Peaches (page 237)

Cranberry and Walnut Dark
Chocolate Bark (page 244)

Frozen Peanut Butter Balls
(page 248)

Gluten-Free

Creamy Cocoa Oatmeal (page 21)

Savory Steel Cut Oatmeal
(page 22)

Stick-with-You Polenta (page 25)

Cinnamon Peach Topping
(page 30)

Mushroom and Spinach Crepes
(page 35)

More-Vegetable-Than-Egg Frittata
(page 36)

Corn Tortilla with Fig Jam and
Roasted Turkey (page 37)

Coconut-Almond Energy Bars
(page 44)

Pumpkin-Cherry Trail Mix
(page 48)

Cinnamon and Sugar Popcorn
(page 49)

Rosemary-Parmesan Popcorn
(page 49)

Roasted Almond Butter (page 51)

Sliced Apple with Goat Cheese
and Balsamic Vinegar (page 52)

Butternut Squash Hummus
(page 54)

Corn-Melon Salsa (page 55)

Good-for-You Black Forest Blizzard
(page 56)

Crunchy Coffee-Cocoa Shake
(page 57)

Maple–Pumpkin Pie Smoothie
(page 57)

Blueberry-Oatmeal Smoothie
(page 58)

Orange-Pomegranate Power
Smoothie (page 60)

Spinach-Kiwi Cooler (page 61)

Cherry-Coconut Recovery Shake
(page 61)

Spinach, Bacon, and Sweet Potato
Salad (page 64)

Chicken Salad with Peas, Feta, and
Mint (page 68)

Tuna Salad with Parsley Dressing
(page 69)

Mint Potato Salad (page 73)

Creamy Coleslaw (page 74)

Fresh Market Slaw (page 75)

Watermelon and Feta Salad
(page 76)

Cantaloupe and Cucumber Salad
(page 77)

Chickpea, Cherry, and Ginger
Salad (page 81)

Greek Lima Bean Salad (page 84)

Honey Dressing (page 85)

Mustard and Cumin Vinaigrette
(page 85)

Nutty Olive Oil Dressing (page 86)

Blackberry Dressing (page 86)

Chilled Zucchini Soup (page 92)

Tomatillo Gazpacho (page 93)

Potato-Leek Soup (page 98)

Celeriac and Potato Soup
(page 99)

Chickpea-Pesto Tomato Soup
(page 100)

Curried Coconut-Squash Soup
(page 102)

Red Lentil and Black Bean Stew
(page 103)

Slow-Cooked Clam Chowder
(page 104)

Creamy Potato-Spinach Soup
(page 105)

Spicy Sausage and Mushroom
Soup (page 109)

Bean and Vegetable Chili
(page 113)

Quick-and-Easy Marinara
(page 138)

Fire-Roasted Meat Sauce
(page 139)

Basil-Mint Pesto (page 141)

Kale-Almond Pesto (page 142)

Cilantro-Pumpkin Pesto
(page 143)

Grilled Beef Fajitas (page 162)

Stove-Top Pork and Brown Rice
(page 171)

Pork Tenderloin with Winter
Vegetables (page 172)

Super-Easy Barbecue Pulled Pork
(page 175)

Chicken Not Pie (page 176)

Red Beans and Rice with Turkey
Sausage (page 185)

Grilled Salmon with Lentil
Tabbouleh (page 188)

Mini Salmon Cakes with Salsa
(page 190)

Salmon Coconut Curry
(page 191)

Spicy Fish Tacos with Pineapple
Slaw (page 193)

Barramundi in Saffron Broth
(page 194)

Maple-Glazed Arctic Char
(page 196)

Sablefish with Pomegranate Syrup
(page 197)

Pacific Halibut with Kiwi Salsa
(page 198)

Garlic Shrimp with White Beans
and Tomatoes (page 200)

Crab-and-Lentil-Stuffed Tomato
with Yogurt Sauce (page 205)

Coconut-Lime Mussels
(page 206)

Brown Rice Salad with Curried
Tofu (page 210)

Chickpea and Spinach Stir-Fry
(page 213)

Dal with Cauliflower, Eggplant,
and Zucchini (page 216)

Steel Cut Oatmeal Risotto with
Asparagus (page 217)

RECITE CONTRIBUTORS

We thank these food writers, chefs, nutritionists, and elite runners, whose work was previously published in Runner's World *and on runnersworld.com.*

Pam Anderson
Multigrain Pancakes
Sweet or Savory Corncakes
Good-for-You Black Forest Blizzard
Tomatillo Gazpacho
Minestrone with Spring Vegetables
Basil-Mint Pesto
Kale-Almond Pesto
Penne with Turkey-Feta Meatballs
Quick 'n' Creamy Chicken Lasagna
Garlic Shrimp with White Beans and Tomatoes
Steamed and Sautéed Sugar Snap Peas
Marinated Peaches
Mocha-Cinnamon Pudding

Liz Applegate, PhD
Hearty Whole Grain Muffins
Awesome Granola
Stick-with-You Polenta
Double Vanilla French Toast
Pumpkin-Cherry Trail Mix
Roasted Almond Butter
Corn Melon Salsa
Orange-Pomegranate Power Smoothie
Immune-Boosting Raspberry-Almond Smoothie
Creamy Coleslaw
Honey Dressing
Nutty Olive Oil Dressing
Thai Avocado Soup
Slow-Cooked Clam Chowder

Wheat Berry and Beef Stew
Roast Beef Pita with Cucumber-Yogurt Sauce
Bean and Shrimp Quesadilla
Marinated Beef and Veggie Kebabs
Meat Loaf
Thai Beef and Snow Pea Stir-Fry
Pork Tenderloin with Winter Vegetables
Marinated Grilled Chicken
Chicken with Asparagus, Mushrooms, and Rice
Swiss Chard with Toasted Quinoa and Tomato
Hearty Red Scalloped Potatoes
Chocolate-Berry Crisp
Chocolate-Oatmeal Cookies
Super Fudgy Brownies
Pumpkin-Pecan Pie

Nate Appleman
Egg and Bean Burrito with Avocado and Yogurt-Lime Sauce
Spiced Pecans
Chicken Stir-Fry with Green Beans and Broccoli
Spicy Fish Tacos with Pineapple Slaw
Chickpea Spread for Bruschetta

Gregg Avedon
Frozen Peanut Butter Balls

Mark Bittman
More-Vegetable-Than-Egg Frittata
Spinach, Bacon, and Sweet Potato Salad
Thai Beef Salad with Mint
Tabbouleh
Bean and Vegetable Chili
Meat and Grain Burgers
Tagliatelle with Peas, Chile, and Mint
Bow-Ties with Tomato and Arugula
Chicken Not Pie
Dal with Cauliflower, Eggplant, and Zucchini

Richard Blais
Beets with Avocado and Orange

Joan Salge Blake, MS, RD, LDN
Pasta Bean Toss

Gesine Bullock-Prado
Hummingbird Muffins
Sliced Apple with Goat Cheese and Balsamic Vinegar
Roasted Pink Grapefruit with Honey Yogurt
Long-Run Cake with Peanut Butter–Cream Cheese Frosting
Sticky Toffee Figgy Cupcakes
Soft Ginger Cookies

Ashley Gartland
Cranberry and Walnut Dark Chocolate Bark

David Santner
Coconut-Almond Energy Bars

Art Smith
Southern Unfried Chicken
Steel Cut Oatmeal Risotto with Asparagus

Nick Symmonds
Red Beans and Rice with Turkey Sausage

Carrie Tollefson
Grilled Beef Fajitas

Rachel Meltzer Warren, MS, RD
Sweet or Savory Popcorn

Patricia Wells
Mushroom and Spinach Crepes
Chicken Salad with Peas, Feta, and Mint
Mint Potato Salad
Watermelon and Feta Salad
Cantaloupe and Cucumber Salad
Chilled Zucchini Soup
Soba Noodles with Chicken and Peanut Sauce

ACKNOWLEDGMENTS

This book would not have been possible without the help of a great number of people. I'd like to start by thanking the 30-plus recipe contributors, who over the years have made *Runner's World* a go-to source for healthy, easy, and delicious meals. In particular, I'd like to thank Liz Applegate, PhD, and Matthew Kadey, MS, RD, who contributed enormously to this book, and Pamela Nisevich Bede, MS, RD, CSSD, LD, who reviewed every recipe and offered her sound nutrition expertise whenever it was needed.

A huge amount of gratitude goes out to the Rodale Test Kitchen—JoAnn Brader, Jennifer Kushnier, and Anne Dewalt. This dedicated team spent hours upon hours reviewing, testing, and editing recipes—and answering lots of questions. Their expertise touches every page.

My editors Stephanie Sun, Mark Weinstein, and Nancy N. Bailey offered invaluable insights that made this book better than I ever thought possible. Christina Gaugler, Mitch Mandel, Adrienne Anderson, and Paige Hicks designed and photographed a gorgeous, mouthwatering cookbook that brings so many of the recipes to life.

I'd like to thank the *Runner's World* staff for their thoughts, ideas, and inspiration—and for being willing to taste recipes even when they were a work in progress. A sincere thanks goes to fellow editors Tish Hamilton and Meghan Loftus for lightening my magazine load when needed, and to our interns, Alissa Hardiman and Kit Fox, who graciously and adeptly handled any cookbook-related task asked of them.

Finally, thank you to my husband, Nate. Without your support, I never would have made it past Chapter 1. And to my son, Owen, and daughter, Nora, who kept me smiling all the way through Chapter 10.

INDEX